Bookmarking

**Recent Titles in the Linworth
Tech Tools for Learning Series**

The Networked Library: A Guide for the Educational Use of Social Networking Sites
Melissa A. Purcell

Bookmarking

Beyond the Basics

ALICIA VANDENBROEK

TECH TOOLS FOR LEARNING SERIES

 LINWORTH

AN IMPRINT OF ABC-CLIO, LLC
Santa Barbara, California • Denver, Colorado • Oxford, England

Library of Congress Cataloging-in-Publication Data

Vandenbroek, Alicia E.
    Bookmarking : beyond the basics / Alicia E. Vandenbroek.
        pages cm. — (Linworth tech tools for learning series)
    Includes bibliographical references and index.
    ISBN 978-1-58683-535-4 (hardcopy : alk. paper) —
ISBN 978-1-58683-536-1 (ebook)   1. Social bookmarking—
Computer programs.   2. Online social networks—Library applications.
3. Internet in school libraries.   4. Internet in education.   I. Title.
    Z674.75.S63V36   2012
    025.04'2—dc23   2012007280

ISBN: 978-1-58683-535-4
EISBN: 978-1-58683-536-1

16 15 14 13 12   1 2 3 4 5

This book is also available on the World Wide Web as an eBook.
Visit www.abc-clio.com for details.

Linworth
An Imprint of ABC-CLIO, LLC

ABC-CLIO, LLC
130 Cremona Drive, P.O. Box 1911
Santa Barbara, California 93116-1911

This book is printed on acid-free paper ∞

Manufactured in the United States of America

Contents

CHAPTER 10: Extending the Basics: LiveBinders Tutorial

79

CHAPTER 11: Practical Application: Putting LiveBinders to Work

87

CHAPTER 12: Web 2.0 Tech Tools Challenge: Diigo Tutorial

97

CHAPTER 13: Practical Application: Putting Diigo to Work

105

CHAPTER 14: Cutting-Edge Bookmarking: QR Codes

115

1

An Introduction to Social Bookmarking

When you think about social bookmarking, what is the first thought that comes to your mind? Are you already familiar with the social bookmarking tools covered in this book and just looking for new techniques for incorporating these strategies in your library or classroom? Perhaps you fall in the middle range and maintain your own bookmarks but aren't quite sure how that translates into student activities or what the difference is between normal bookmarks and social bookmarks. Or, you might be at the other end of the spectrum and not even feel comfortable creating a bookmark on your computer. Wherever you find yourself today, be confident that together we will sift through the world of social bookmarking and create a manageable way to arrange your personal bookmarks. Mastering these skills and advancing to the next level means combining bookmarking skills with the content-rich component of social networking. Social networking is a powerful enrichment tool that bolsters both your curriculum and library program.

A simple definition of bookmarking is: marking a website on your computer so that you can quickly access it for later use. Think breadcrumb shortcuts back to the village if you were Hansel and Gretel. In the past, keeping up with bookmarks required bookmarking the same sites multiple times on every computer you used; or inevitably you'd have the bookmark you needed at home instead of at work, or vice versa. Today, bookmarking is far more convenient. Logging into a bookmarking website gives you on-the-go access to your links anywhere you have Internet access.

If you combine this type of continual access bookmarking with the collaborative aspect, social bookmarking in its most basic form allows users to share Internet links, for both easy access and convenience. This is different from file sharing, in that the individual is only providing the link to the website rather than providing the files. Many social bookmarking sites allow you to annotate pages to add personal notes and/or tag pages by giving a one-word hint about what the link involves, allowing quick sorting for later reference and individual customization. The ability to share these bookmarks means that it no longer requires endless hours of researching those perfect bookmarks, because you can collaborate with your peers. This form of collaboration expands your reach, allowing you to interact with anyone in the country—or even around the world—who has similar interests.

The days are over when students had to type in long websites that accidentally took them to wrong websites. Also gone is the need for linking to websites from a Word document in a central location. Social bookmarking allows easy access to links as well as a way to learn and share collaboratively. This book is a journey into some social bookmarking tools that, if used thoughtfully, can impact a school's library, classroom instruction, and a public library's program. Regardless of your prior background, the following chapters will help you learn and develop your skills with a practical step-by-step approach. For convenience, there is one chapter devoted to the ins and outs of using each specific bookmarking tool and then a subsequent chapter that showcases ways to put this bookmarking tool to work in your library. Some applications will focus more on education approaches, while others will focus on personal or community-building projects, so both are included. One helpful tip to remember as you explore the bookmarking sites is that even though an idea is presented in the book under a specific bookmarking website, most ideas are easily adapted to whatever site you are most comfortable with using. Even if a project doesn't appear directly applicable to your profession, take a moment and peek at the activity. Sometimes, the best ideas come from "stealing" an idea and reinventing it to suit your own individual needs.

Another potential area of diversity is that educational settings have different limitations on Web access. Some schools and even public libraries have filters that lock down Web 2.0 technology to the point of crippling it, while others allow broader access and leave guardianship of students and patrons to the librarian. When reading and trying the activities in this book, always process the material in relationship to how you can directly apply it. Sometimes, it is simply a matter of educating those in charge of the filter. Emerging social bookmarking tools take off so quickly that the guard dogs of the filter don't have a chance to respond. If you build appropriate and educational programs that legitimately enhance curriculum, most administrators will reconsider allowing access if they can see the benefit. As with other Web 2.0 technology, educators sit uniquely positioned between protecting privacy and still enriching curriculum. That balancing act tips different directions, depending on administration. Use what you can when you can but continue the education process, because education is the key to student success.

Browsers

The steps in this tutorial may look slightly different from my examples, depending on which browser you use. The tutorials were created using Firefox. Some of the social bookmarking tools allow placement of shortcuts on the toolbars. Simplify your life later by updating your browser to the most current version before getting too far into this tutorial. That allows you to get used to where things are without changing the layout.

Bookmark Toolbar

Before we begin, make sure your bookmarking toolbar shows up on your browser. If this is a new term: a browser is what you open when you search the Internet. Examples include: Internet Explorer, Safari, Firefox, Google Chrome, and so on. It can be a little confusing to give step-by-step directions, because there are so many versions of different browsers, so following are the four most-used browsers.

If you aren't sure if you have the bookmark toolbar showing, follow the steps below. You can show or hide the toolbar as many times as you like until you are familiar with what it looks like and where it goes. This is important because during the tutorials you will create shortcuts by dragging buttons to this toolbar. This shortcut makes bookmarking easier, because you bookmark with one click rather than opening several different windows.

If you aren't a huge bookmarker, you may not know that when you are on a website you like you can simply click and drag the website anywhere on this bookmark bar, creating a bookmark. Typically, most people only do this for their 10–15 most frequently used bookmarks. Those steps only bookmark websites on that specific computer. You would repeat that process on any other computer you use or, better yet, just bookmark them using a social bookmarking site!

Throughout the following discussion, when terms are capitalized and bold, that indicates that they are command options in the browser.

Firefox

On the newest version of Firefox, the toolbar is typically under **Options**. Verify that the phrase "bookmark toolbar" shows a check next to it. If running an older version, the bookmark toolbar is made visible by using **View** and then **Toolbars**.

Internet Explorer

From the menu at the top of the browser select **View**, **Toolbars**, and then **Favorites Bar**.

Safari

Click on the triangle next to the small wheel in the top-right corner. Next click **Show Bookmarks Bar**. Note: if the bookmark bar is already running, this will say **Hide Bookmarks Bar**. Do not click it, in that case.

Google Chrome

On the right hand side select the wrench icon. Next click on **Bookmark** and then **Show Bookmark Toolbar**.

Exporting Bookmarks

If you have a substantial number of bookmarks on your computer already, exporting them from your browser is beneficial because it facilitates adding them in a bulk add; all at one time, rather than starting from scratch. If you do not have bookmarks or only have a handful, skip this step. Personally, my bookmarks were so disorganized when I started this process that it was just easier to start from scratch. Also, consider deleting any personal bookmarks that would give away too much personal information, such as your bank. Think about it and then, if you want to export your bookmarks, follow these steps:

Firefox

- From the Menu bar select **Bookmarks** and then **Show all bookmarks**.
- Click **Import** and **Backup.**
- Click **Export HTML**.
- When the **Save as Window** comes up, choose where to save the file. This is an important step, because you want to know where to find the files later. Typically, the desktop is a good location for short-term storage. Change the file name to include the date, in case you add other bookmarks and need to make a new document.
- The document is saved as an .html document. It isn't a bad idea to back up your bookmarks once in a while so that you have another copy.

Internet Explorer

- From the Menu Bar, select **File** and then **Import** and **Export**.
- Choose **Export to a file**.
- Choose **Favorites**. If you use feeds, also select those.
- Choose the file you want to export. Typically, this is your Favorites folder.
- Click **Browse**.
- When the **Save as Window** comes up, choose where to save the file. This is an important step because you want to know where to find the files later. Typically, the desktop is a good location for short-term storage. Change the file name to include the date, in case you add other bookmarks and need to make a new document.
- The document is saved as an .html document. It isn't a bad idea to back up your bookmarks once in a while so that you have another copy.

Safari

- From the Menu Bar click **File**. If the menu bar is hidden, you can make it visible as you did the bookmark toolbar. Click on the little wheel in the top-right corner and select **Show Menu Bar**.

- Select **Export Bookmarks**.

- When the **Save as Window** comes up, choose where to save the file. This is an important step because you want to know where to find the files later. Typically, the desktop is a good location for short-term storage. Change the file name to include the date, in case you add other bookmarks and need to make a new document.

- The document is saved as an .html document. It isn't a bad idea to back up your bookmarks once in a while so that you have another copy.

Google Chrome

- On the right-hand side select the wrench icon.

- Select **Bookmarks**.

- Select **Bookmark Manager**.

- Select **Organize**.

- Select **Export Bookmarks to HTML File**.

- When the **Save as Window** comes up, choose where to save the file. This is an important step because you want to know where to find the files later. Typically, the desktop is a good location for short-term storage. Change the file name to include the date, in case you add other bookmarks and need to make a new document.

- The document is saved as an .html document. It is a good idea to back up your bookmarks once in a while so that you have another copy.

Personal Accounts and Professional Accounts

When you consider social bookmarks, your first administrative decision is determining whether you want one account for all your bookmarks, or two. For simplicity sake, some people have their personal and work information all in one account. Some individuals like more privacy, so they maintain two separate accounts. Another option is to have one account for your library or classroom. Most social networking accounts require an e-mail for activation. Use a generic Gmail e-mail account that you create for school registration. There is no right or wrong answer to the number of accounts you choose to have, only personal preference.

Student Accounts

The next tough decision is what to do about the student e-mail needed for creation of individual student accounts. Some school districts have access to individual school e-mails and some do not. Jim Holland addresses some ways to work around these in his handout *Issues with Web 2.0* (http://webapplications.wikispaces.com/). Here are some options if students do not have e-mail accounts:

No student account: After considering the options with your administration and teaching colleagues a decision to not allow student accounts may be appropriate for your campus. This does not need to be set in stone. As students show they can use the technology responsibly, try to revisit this topic with fresh eyes.

Gmail: Have students set up accounts on Gmail. This is a free service provided by Google.

Piggyback e-mail: To do this set up a generic Gmail account. Ex. yourschoollibrary@gmail.com. For student accounts, students can use their student id, a + sign, and then your school e-mail. Ex: student1+yourschoollibrary@gmail.com. If working with younger children, you may want to set this up in advance if you need password control. If students are sharing a log on, make sure they do not delete the work of other students. Typically, e-mails are required only if passwords are forgotten.

Fake e-mail: When registering for an account you can simply make up a fake e-mail address. This only works for sites that do not require e-mail confirmation. One problem with not using an actual e-mail address is that if you forget your e-mail there is no way to retrieve your information.

Cross Connections between Social Bookmarking Ideas

This book highlights different ideas for each social bookmarking website. Please remember that these ideas are not limited to the social bookmarking tool exclusively. What works on one website can typically be adapted to other websites.

I've been teaching technology classes long enough to know that individuals who are uncomfortable with technology hit the frustration level must faster than do those who are comfortable with technology. As you learn about these new sites, don't feel like you have to master them all right away. Choose one to start, and then develop your skills at a rate that feels comfortable to you. If possible, work in a collaborative setting. If you divide up the work between other librarians or other members of your campus, it will not only provide you other people to share ideas with but also give you a touchstone if you have questions or get stuck. Remember, most of these websites have great tutorials or blogs where people have probably asked the exact questions on your mind. If not, someone is probably thinking about that same questions, so jump out there and ask. Two other sources for help can be found on YouTube videos (http://www.youtube.com/) and on 5min videos (http://www.5min.com).

Technology Requirements and Restrictions

Because social bookmarking tools are Internet based, they require a device with Internet capability. These can be computers, laptops, netbooks, iPod touches, smart phones, or iPads. When additional technology beyond one of these is required, it will be denoted in the overview of the lesson. Another consideration is that, due to filtering issues, websites bookmarked at home may not work at school. Work with your Technology Department or even your Curriculum Department when you find that sites with solid educational value are blocked. If you meet with opposition, illustrate how the skill supports the library's goals or the school district's goals. In most cases, sites are blocked due to a generic rule and staff members are flexible about exceptions once the rationale is clear.

If your library has access to a SMART board or other such technology, using these websites in the library is even easier, because the whole class can participate at one time. These are only mentioned and not more fully discussed because not all schools—and even fewer public libraries—have access to this technology.

Costs

Just as with other sites you've used, most Web 2.0 sites have several different levels of usage. The full versions of the sites discussed are sometimes subscription based and require a monthly or yearly charge. Subscribing to these sites is not necessary unless there is a tool you desperately want that you don't have access to under the free or educational version. All the sites covered in this book have a free version with almost all the same features at no cost. You primarily lose some of the monitoring capabilities; meaning that you can't see who and where your links are being used. The paid versions also typically remove ads. Most of these sites recognize the audience using their product and, as a result, ads are usually safe, even for the younger elementary audience. Additionally, some sites have a middle level for educators and provide an account level that is more than the free but still less than the subscription. When registering for an account, check on the website for educator discounts, if those apply to you. Growing websites add more of these types of features based on user feedback. If you do create an educational account, use it responsibly. For example, I have two Animoto accounts, one for my personal use that I pay for and one for school, because making videos for my family would not be appropriate using my school account. That is what you agree to when you read the small print.

Password Tracker

As you begin setting up accounts for these social bookmarking sites, you may end up with different usernames and passwords. This information management can become slightly overwhelming. Here are a few organizational options:

- Allow your computer to remember your password. This is not a good option to use when sharing a computer, because anyone who uses your computer will have access to your passwords.

- There are many sites that track passwords online for free. I'm always reluctant to store that data online, for fear of them getting accidentally released to the public. Even seemingly secure sites can fall victim to hackers.

- Use a spreadsheet password tracker on your computer. This can be kept locally or stored in the Cloud (on a site like http://dropbox.com). Worksheet 8 has a Password Tracker that is easily modified to fit your needs.

- Use a paper copy of a spreadsheet that you keep with you so you always have your password.

- Create an OpenID account. More and more sites allow account creation with this log in, instead of your creating a separate account.

Flash Websites

As you build social bookmarking websites, you will notice that some of these websites use Flash and some do not. Flash is the program that runs behind the scenes, animating the websites. When using devices that support Flash, some of your items will not display properly. Currently, none of the iPods, iPhones, or iPads support Flash, nor is that likely to change in the future. You can work around that by downloading a browser that allows you to view Flash websites, such as CloudBrowse, or using an app like Rover. Unfortunately, most of these are not free and none display the website perfectly. Some websites are working around that by building non-Flash alternative pages and some are building applications as work-arounds. As the tablet market expands, this should be less of an issue for libraries.

Posting Student/Patron Work

Best practice involves getting permission in writing before posting work created by a student or patron, in order to reduce liability and respect intellectual property. Sometimes, this permission is a part of the paperwork a student and parent fills out at the start of the school year, but that varies from district to district. A public library can be a little more flexible about this, but anytime a minor creates the content, it is best to get written permission from both the parent and the student before publishing the work. A modifiable sample of permission is included as Worksheet 7. Depending on the audience, it may be necessary to add a caveat about the author having the responsibility for insuring intellectual property rules are followed.

Privacy Settings

Privacy settings are unique to each location. I would love to work at a school that says, "Let's take out your phones and get to work," but I don't. We are slowly catching up to the digital age, but it hasn't been easy. As an academic or a public librarian, determining how much to lock down the privacy setting on accounts is up to you. Some sites give you complete control in the free version, while some only provide that flexibility in the paid version. Depending on your audience and privacy concerns, different levels are appropriate for each situation.

Checking Out Devices

Several times in this book, we discuss using a variety of devices such as computers, iPods, iPads, and so forth. That inevitably brings up the question of technology management. In schools, this is typically done on a class-by-class basis, checking out the supplied technology to the teacher; however, there are many schools that assign technology barcodes and students check out the technology much like they would a book. Ultimately, this decision is up to you as a librarian, but take time for consultation with your library and technology committees for best practices and practical input. Involving others in these types of decisions will help encourage collaboration within your school. Ultimately, these items come from your grants or your library budget and you know your end user better than anyone else might. That said, I would challenge you to move past your comfort zone, if you are willing. Given the chance, people usually surprise you in a good way if the expectations are clear and the policies are well thought out and made clear to everyone. The key lies in preparation and training. Make sure that patrons know your expectations and also know that you really do check that items are returned in the same condition. Where there is accountability there is responsibility—in most cases.

Common Core Standards

Because state requirement vary from state to state, this book uses the Common Core Standards (http://www.corestandards.org/). Sometimes, the notation is only the basic Anchor Standard and sometimes the specific standard is listed. This is due to the specificity of the project. Feel free to delineate these further as you specify your relative grade level and specific content.

Share What You Learn

While this book focuses primarily on librarians, please share what you learn with teachers and administrators, perhaps even parents. Even if teachers and colleagues only initially use social bookmarking for personal use, they will love you for taking the time to show them new ways to bookmark. It never ceases to amaze me how many teachers and professionals are still typing in very long Web addresses or using Google because they don't know of a better way for saving and sharing information. Use social bookmarking with students around teachers, but also help them one-on-one so they can apply social bookmarking in their lives.

Copyright in Education

This probably applies to very few of you, but just a reminder that most schools have very clear guidelines on ownership of creative materials. Most school districts have intellectual property rules in the district guidelines that state that anything created during school hours, with school equipment, or added to district documents, typically belongs to the school district. For example, if I choose to share content I've created in curriculum documents, it becomes the property of the school district. When this is policy is violated, it can become a copyright issue, because even though you create it, you do not own the rights to the material; the school district does.

As we model the ethical use of information with our students and peers, it is mandatory that any content used should provide full attribution or citation. If we don't practice the skills we teach, students will not think that these ethical rules really matter. As a classroom teacher, I unintentionally violated copyright law all the time until I learned more about it, thanks to a librarian's example. Now that I'm a librarian myself, I monitor that closely. It's not always easy, but it is essential.

Citing Projects Using EasyBib

If you aren't familiar with the website EasyBib (http://easybib.com), I will tell you that it is tremendous! I was able to complete a works cited page for 16 books and 2 databases in less than 10 minutes. Students use their collection of information on websites, books, newspapers, journals, databases, and more; modify the citation information as appropriate for the project; and then create a final Works Cited

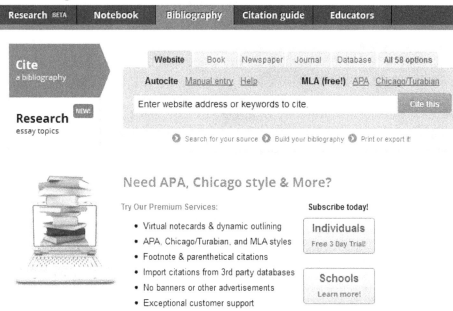

citation. Once all the resources are added, students can transform citations into a Word document format with the push of a button or save for later. EasyBib will cite MLA and APA styles for free, and Chicago and Turabian with the purchased version.

EasyBib is different from other online citation tools because it contains a collection of resources with complete citations. This means that students can look up books or other items they used for research and add any unique information, such as page numbers, before creating the citation, but they do not have to type in all the citation information. EasyBib makes it very easy to find resources. In most cases, students use titles, though with books, I encourage ISBNs, when possible.

There is a paid version of EasyBib but the free version is very powerful. EasyBib provides student handouts and video clips showcasing their product, if you need extra support.

Because citation is essential in everything involving social bookmarking, here is a quick tutorial on EasyBib when creating your own citations:

Step 1: Go to http://easybib.com/

Registration is not required for creation of a citation, but if you plan to work on multiple computers, or multiple users will be using the same computer, you may want to create a free account.

Step 2: Choose the item you are citing.

The most commonly used types of citations are listed in the tabs. If your item is not shown, click on the last option to show all 58 options and make your selection.

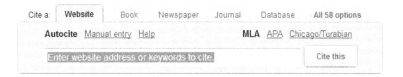

Step 3: Choose your Citation Manual tool.

EasyBib defaults to MLA 7. If you need a different citation tool, simply click on the name at the top of the screen. MLA and APA are part of the free version.

Step 4: Choose Manual Citation.

The reason I cite with manual citation rather than their standard citation is that it allows me to quickly change anything I need to, as well as add my own citations.

Step 5: Find your item.

Cite a Book Help   MLA 6 **MLA 7** APA Chicago/Turabian

Just fill out what you know. We'll format it correctly.

Search for your book: [   ]   [Autocite!]

New! Search by book title, keywords, or ISBN! powered by ⑤ WorldCat

Medium: **In print**   Website   Online database   Other (ebook)   ◂ [Choos⋅

Citing: [The whole book   ▾]

Contributors: [Author ▾]   [   ]   [   ]   [   ]   Remove
                            First   MI   Last / corp.

                                                    + Add another contributor

In print publication info

Source title: [   ]

Advanced info: [   ]   [   ]   [   ]
                 Vol.   Edition   Series

Publication info: [   ]   [   ]   [   ]
                    Publisher   City   Year

[Add Annotation]

[Create Citation]

Once the EasyBib search box comes up, type in the box to locate the record. You can search by title, keywords, or ISBN. Type the title in and hit **enter**. A list of books will appear below the search box. Choose the correct one by clicking **Select**.

The program will then auto-fill the boxes below. Make any changes or accept the citation as is. Don't forget to look at the citing that defaults to the entire book. Change this if you only want to reference part of a book. Click **Add Annotation**, if needed. If not, click **Create Citation**.

The book whisperer: awakening the inner reader in every child   [Select »]
Donalyn Miller - Jeff Anderson - Jossey-Bass - 2009
More about this source » Find at your local library through WorldCat »

Step 6: Create your Works Cited page.

The new citation will appear on the screen. You can repeat this process for all items needing citation. When finished, you can save for later, save as a Google doc, or print as a Word document. When you got to the print option, it looks like you have to register in order to print, but choose **Click to Continue** without registration, if desired.

The final works cited page will appear in Word almost instantly. You can save this to your desktop, USB flash drive, or e-mail to yourself. Use cut and paste if you want to include in an existing Word document.

Step 7: Other Features

- Research-brand new search engine in beta testing. This allows searching of both academic and nonacademic topics.

- Notecards—a wonderful feature but only in the paid premium version. Subscription is per user, so it varies by school or library.

- Citation Guide—tips for MLA or APA citation formats.

- Help section—lots of handouts, tutorials, and tips. Be sure to take a peek at the librarian and educators link. There are powerful resources for students, teachers, and librarians.

2

Starting off Simple:
Delicious Tutorial

Have you ever been working at school and wished you could remember that great site you found last night on your home computer? Delicious is an easy-to-use bookmarking tool that lets you do that and so much more. Simply put, Delicious makes locating websites incredibly easy. The social component comes in because you can also view the bookmarks of a network of professionals or friends; also known as a followers. Let's face it: in today's world, a new great website or wiki is created every hour. Sharing resources is the way to learn about new resources and create contacts quickly, thus simplifying your life and reducing the need to sit at the computer hour after hour looking for new resources.

Delicious is one of the most commonly known social bookmarking sites. Users were devastated in the fall of 2010 to learn that Delicious was scheduled for sunsetting by Yahoo! In early 2011, users were delighted, however, with the announcement that Yahoo! wasn't canceling the site but selling it to Chad Hurley and Steve Chen, the founders of YouTube. Hurley and Chen are combining Delicious with their new company AVOS.

In September 2011, Delicious went live with its new look and features. If you did not agree to AVOS' terms and conditions prior to this conversion, it is possible that you lost access to your account and may need to create a new account. Delicious will be in beta status initially as AVOS continues to monitor the site and add additional features. They willingly accept user feedback, so feel free to make suggestions or comments. The new layout is much more clean and very easy to navigate. For more information or for updates on Delicious changes, see the AVOS website (http://avos.com/).

Step 1: Create an Account

Go to the Delicious website http://www.delicious.com/.
Click **join**. join

Complete the account registration.

join now and get stacking

delicious ID

between 3 and 32 characters

password

6 character minimum including numbers or symbols

email

by clicking "join" you are indicating that you have read and agree to the terms of service.

join

... or login

Once you've created an account, Delicious will suggest adding the bookmarklet directly to your browser. This is not required, but I would highly suggest adding the bookmarklet, as it makes saving links a breeze. The bookmarklet tool is slightly easier to use than the browser extensions, because you do not have to worry the browser being updated.

If you would prefer the browser extensions, those are located under the Tools link. Be sure to install the correct extensions for the browser you are currently using. Without getting too technical, an extension is designed to work with a specific Web browser to improve performance with a specific application. For more information on extensions and Delicious refer to the Delicious help page (http://www.delicious.com/help).

Step 2: Settings and Importing Links

Click on **My Links**. Note: in the old Delicious these were called bookmarks, but the new Delicious calls these links. This is a drop-down menu directly under your user name.

my links

my stacks

following

settings

logout

Upload a photo and add any desired information like an e-mail address or website URL. This is also where you can change your password.

Import Bookmarks (If Desired)

In the settings screen, add bookmarks or backup your links.

import / upload links
Transfer a copy of the link
inside your browser.

export / backup links
Download a copy of your links
for safe-keeping or to transfer
into your browser.

delete profile pic

delete account

Step 3: Add a New Link

As you navigate the Internet, locate a website that you would like to add to Delicious. Click the **Save on Delicious** bookmarklet. Add appropriate tags, comments, and mark as private if desired. Delicious does allow multi-word tags. Be sure to save the link.

save link

Once you've saved you link, it will appear on the **My Links** screen. Access this by clicking on **My Links** in the drop-down menu under your user name.

28 sep 11   ☐   6179 saves

The Site for Books & Readers - Shelfari

http://www.shelfari.com/

Step 4: Creating and Managing Stacks

When you are finished adding links, create a stack to keep them organized. Creating a stack involves selecting the various links that you want to combine. Three links are the minimum requirement for a stack.

28 sep 11   3 saves

Good Reads

http://www.goodreads.com/videos

Book trailers

28 sep 11   219 saves

BTFA Home

http://booktrailersforall.com/

book trailers

28 sep 11   50 saves

Book Trailers - Adolescent Movies for Literacy!

http://www.homepages.dsu.edu/mgeary/booktrailers/adolescent.htm

book trailers

Click **Create Stack**.   create stack

There are several different view options, depending on what you like best. You can add a photo if you'd like and then publish your stack. Stacks can be edited at any time and are public.

7 links   grid view   list view   full view

Step 5: Following and Inbox

As you look around Delicious, watch for individuals who are bookmarking items that you find interesting. Locate their profile and then select the **Follow** button. Your inbox is where other Delicious users can send you links or messages.

3

Practical Application:
Putting Delicious to Work

When working with other professionals, Delicious is the most commonly used social bookmarking site. Appendices included with this book reference worksheets and rubrics that will serve as templates or suggestions to use as you create your own working documents. Worksheet 1 is a sample electronic lesson plan. Storing lesson plans electronically allows easy collaboration and a greener file management system.

Personal Use

Delicious is a great way to keep up with your bookmark collection so that you have access on every computer you use. Because it has been around for longer than a few of the other social bookmarking sites, the base of users is substantial. I use multiple computers at school, as well as when I work on library material at home. Using Delicious means you have 24/7 access to all of your bookmarks, with minimal extra work. I do maintain one account for my personal bookmarks and one account for my library, so that I can have my personal links readily available.

Using Delicious in an Academic Setting

Lesson/Activity: Promote Reading Lists with Students

Common Core Standards: n/a

Overview: Create a Delicious account for your library or classroom. Rather than bookmarking links on a website or wiki, bookmark sites in Delicious. Create a stack for reading lists. Provide reading lists for the age of students you teach as well as for ages below and above. This will help capture your reluctant readers as well as help parents locate resources for themselves or for younger siblings. The more comfortable students are going to your lists, the more they will view you as an authority in research. Also add a reading list for professional development suggestions for teachers. These can be books in your collection or just general suggestions.

Required Preparation: Create an account for your library, bookmark websites.

Additional Technology Requirements: none

Tips and Suggestions: When creating your lists, be sure to consult the district's curriculum guides. They will include resources that they expect students to use that aren't on your booklist radar.

Worksheets/Rubrics: n/a

Lesson/Activity: Professional Collaboration

Common Core Standards: n/a

Overview: Either establish a shared Delicious account for librarians within your district, or help librarians set up accounts to share your links and contribute their own. Depending on the size of your district, this can include all librarians or, in larger districts, simply librarians who teach the same age range. Set up links to resources to enhance professional development. Some examples include: book review sites, websites or wikis that promote technology, links to popular authors, lesson plan ideas, and so on. Sharing links provides collaborative opportunities without having to leave the library, and creating a stack is the perfect way to collaborate with other professionals.

Required Preparation: Create Delicious accounts, initial tabs and bookmarks, promotion with other professionals.

Additional Technology Requirements: none

Tips and Suggestions: Include instructional facilitators if applicable as an added benefit to your collection of resources. Like librarians, these instructional partners do not have a team to meet with during the school day and can feel isolated. If the person who leads instruction at your school sees you as vital to instruction, it will potentially mean more collaborative opportunities.

Worksheets/Rubrics: n/a

Lesson/Activity: Using Delicious in Research via Tags

Common Core Standards: Integration of Knowledge and Ideas 8 and 9 and Research to Build and Present Knowledge 7–9.

Overview: Before research begins, have a mini-lesson on what a tag is and how it is used. Ehow has tutorials and videos on tags (http://tinyurl.com/3vw7eb3) and 5min has a short introduction to tags and key words for older students or adults (http://tinyurl.com/3hmwchu). Help students understand how tags are similar to Boolean searching. Review with students how to determine the validity of a website and if it is appropriate for their research projects. When students begin researching, guide them through creating their own accounts in Delicious. As they bookmark websites on their topic of research, review tagging. As they begin to bookmark sites, they can view other users who have similar tags and add those websites to theirs, if they are appropriate. Students can join their teacher's Delicious account and as they research, the teacher can spot-check links, sending individual messages to students if any problems arise. Use the stack feature to combine similar tags.

Required Preparation: Show students how to create their own accounts and explain tagging. Help the teacher set up a Delicious account and get familiar with the way Delicious works.

Additional Technology Requirements: none

Tips and Suggestions: If students are working in groups, they can follow those individuals with the same topic. To ensure everyone is working, consider tagging with the name of who created the link or by ensuring that all group members had links before sharing information.

Worksheets/Rubrics: n/a

Lesson/Activity: Support Resources for Parents of Special Education or English as a Second Language (ESL)

Common Core Standards: n/a

Details: Create two different lists of bookmarks for parents of students in special education and ESL. Provide parents with information on student and parents' rights, as well as tips to help their child succeed in school. Include community support groups or programs that parents might not be familiar with. For ESL parents, provide tips for adjusting to school and communicating with the teacher. If your campus offers translation services, make sure to include this information in the languages that are appropriate for your campus.

Required Preparation: Locate and bookmark links.

Additional Technology Requirements: none

Tips and Suggestions: Keep in mind that, sometimes, parents in these categories have had negative prior experiences with the school system. As you receive feedback or questions, make sure to adjust your links to include this new information. Parents new to this country may not know where they can get free Internet and computer usage. Help them locate those services if your school does not prove them to parents.

Worksheets/Rubrics: n/a

Lesson/Activity: Professional Required Reading for Teachers and Staff

Common Core Standards: n/a

Details: Each campus has different policies on required professional reading. Some campuses have a required non-fiction book every six weeks and some require no outside professional reading at all. To help faculty members stay lifelong learners, provide opportunities for professional reading and collaboration with peers. Professional Learning Communities are an important part of continuing education. Helping your campus develop a Professional Learning Community helps increase awareness of the services your library offers and fosters the idea that libraries are an indispensable part of the educational process. Help your principal locate and share sites that promote topics relevant to your campus needs. Include topics at an introductory level as well as a mastery level. Some examples of topics include:

- Classroom management
- Motivating students
- Reluctant readers
- Using technology for instruction
- Lesson Plan suggestions
- Emerging research on education
- The relationship between libraries and test scores
- Evaluation tips
- Parent relations
- Meeting the needs of different types of students (see where test scores indicate deficiencies)
- Web 2.0 skills

Required Preparation: Locate links and create stacks.

Additional Technology Requirements: none

Tips and Suggestions: Add a separate section for teachers who are working on their Master's or Doctorate degrees. Include links to the databases provided by the district as well as citation information. Many teachers do not know about EasyBib (http://easybib.com) and this can be a real time-saving tool for them.

Worksheets/Rubrics: n/a

Lesson/Activity: Free Online Math Tools

Common Core Standards: Mathematical Practice—Use appropriate tools strategically.

Details: This activity is easily adapted for students of any age. Look for free online tools for students. These can be tutorial sites, online calculators, geometrical shapes, graphing, math fact practice sites, and so on. Also include logic strategy sites, as they promote higher-order thinking skills. If desired, link to a Google Document where students can log on and record their success.

Required Preparation: Locate links and bookmark.

Additional Technology Requirements: none

Tips and Suggestions: Incorporate vertical alignment by collaborating with librarians at feeder campuses. For example, elementary librarians can share resources with middle school and junior high for remediation, and middle schools and junior highs can share resources with elementary for extension. Sharing information means more information for students with minimal work.

Worksheets/Rubrics: n/a

Lesson/Activity: Text Creator Websites

Common Core Standards: Language Progressive Skill L3.3a.

Details: Help students familiarize themselves with navigating between different bookmarks on Delicious by allowing students to move back and forth between different text creator websites previously bookmarked in Delicious. This will help students learn how to locate bookmarks as well as give them an opportunity to incorporate classroom ideas. Bookmark sites that allow student creation of word pictures. Two examples of these websites are Wordle (http://www.wordle.net/) and Tagxedo (http://www.tagxedo.com). In Tagxedo, you control the shape and can even add images. These require a lot of words but they are a creative way to introduce yourself, discuss a character, list parts of speech, and so on. This type of word arrangement is called a *word cloud.* A great way to teach tags is allowing students to create and share word clouds of an already created website. Frequently used words will show up in a larger font. These are the best tags for that website since the words are used most often on that site.

Required Preparation: Locate and bookmark websites.

Additional Technology Requirements: none

Tips and Suggestions: Consider making a Tagxedo to advertise your library in a newsletter and then provide the link to the Delicious bookmarks for parents and students to create their own. This is also a fun way to show off all the books you read during the school year.

Worksheets/Rubrics: n/a

Lesson/Activity: Origami and Paper Airplane Tutorials

Common Core Standards: Math 8.G if focusing on translation, rotation, reflection.

Details: Origami is fun, yet frustrating at any age. Create a list of bookmarks tagged with the term "origami." In the same list, or on a separate list, add paper airplanes. Sometimes, science and engineering classes use these as examples of lift and thrust, but books on paper airplanes are not always available in advanced academic library collections. Providing easy to access sites is a way to supplement collections. If possible, find a variety of skill levels and, when possible, video examples, because sometimes Origami directions are confusing if there are a lot of steps. If filtering limits access to already created tutorials, consider filming students and uploading those videos to edu.glogster, as that is typically not blocked. Origami is a fun way to get your math department into the library, because origami shapes illustrate translation, rotation, and reflection.

Required Preparation: Locate and bookmark websites.

Additional Technology Requirements: none

Tips and Suggestions: Consider creating a list for teachers on foldables for classroom use. One example is Dinah Zike (http://www.dinah.com/).

Worksheets/Rubrics: n/a

Using Delicious in a Public Library Setting

Service/Activity: Tax Preparation Tips for Patrons

Community Connection: Provide Internet resources next to tax materials in the library. Coordinate with the Volunteer Income Tax Assistance Program to arrange tax help for patrons who qualify and sign up in advance. See their website for more information (www.irs.gov).

Overview: During tax season, most libraries have tax materials available for patron retrieval. Providing a list of tax preparation websites at this location and on the library website will help patrons who need additional information. Using a business card template in Microsoft Word, provide the link to where the bookmarks are listed on Delicious. Give information on the free service and allow patrons to schedule appointments at the library.

Required Preparation: Collect bookmarks and create cards.

Additional Technology Requirements: none

Tips and Suggestions: If there isn't a volunteer service in the immediate area, most volunteers would be willing to travel if they could schedule multiple appointments at one time. Contact them in advance to discuss your intentions and scheduling tips.

Worksheets/Rubrics: Worksheet 2: Sample Tax Link Cards.

Service/Activity: Stack Competition

Community Connection: Hold a contest between Reference Librarians, where patrons select the winner.

Overview: Each reference librarian in the library creates Delicious accounts to share with the public. On their accounts, they bookmark anything that they think will be of interest to the community. These links can connect to authors, books, research, fun websites, and so on. Post these links on the library website via the stack view. Patrons view the website and vote for the reference librarian they feel has the best links. Building relationships electronically will sometimes help build relationships in the real world. Clever librarians will realize that they can share their competitor's links to make their own site more robust. Patrons can also suggest sites for inclusion. All's fair in contests and social bookmarking.

Required Preparation: Create a delicious account and bookmark websites. Create an online poll for voting.

Additional Technology Requirements: none

Tips and Suggestions: Consider using a tool like SurveyTool (www.surveytool.com/) or Survey Monkey (http://surveymonkey.com) to create the voting tool.

Worksheets/Rubrics: n/a

Service/Activity: Websites for Clerical Skills (Typing and 10 Key)

Community Connection: Arrange for a local temporary agency to visit the library and facilitate a discussion on the opportunities in the clerical profession.

Overview: Keyboarding and 10 Key used to be taught in high school but now that is primarily taught in elementary school and the emphasis varies from campus to campus. With changes in the job market, people need skills that they didn't think were a priority before, such as typing, data entry, and using professional tools such as Microsoft Office. Ask a local temporary agency to speak about openings in the clerical profession and then provide patrons with an opportunity to practice their keyboarding skills.

Required Preparation: Arrange speaker, locate and bookmark websites.

Additional Technology Requirements: none

Tips and Suggestions: If the court reporting market in your community has a lot of opportunities, you might ask a representative from a court reporting school to visit at the same time.

Worksheets/Rubrics: n/a

Service/Activity: List of Resources for Disabled Patrons and Caregivers

Community Connection: n/a

Overview: Use Delicious as a method of supporting disabled patrons. Collect resources on support groups, background on their disability, new emerging research, services offered by the community, services offered by the library, resources for family members or care givers, and so on. Include resources for the visually impaired, because new assistive technology will make that accessible and sometimes it is the family who needs the resources, not just the disabled individual.

Required Preparation: Locate and bookmark links.

Additional Technology Requirements: none

Tips and Suggestions: If you are having trouble locating authoritative sites, coordinate with local service agencies. Most of these foundations and organizations also have helpful links on their websites that you can customize to meet the needs of your patrons.

Worksheets/Rubrics: n/a

Service/Activity: Teacher Collaboration to Promote Educational Materials

Community Connection: Teacher mini-workshop to highlight educations resources.

Overview: This is a simple way to get teachers reluctant to new technology comfortable with Delicious, and at the same time educate them on the services the public library has to offer educators. Teachers are frequently unaware of the services offered by the public library, which can include:

- Library Cards for Non-Residents: if your library participates in a share program where teachers who don't live in the school district can still have library card in that city, make sure to sell this idea to teachers. Many times teachers visit only the library where they live. While this is fabulous, it is also important that teachers are familiar with the local resources so that they can promote them to students.

- Public Library and School Collaborations: if your policies allow, make sure that you are on the volunteer list for local schools. This will allow you to assist with special events and become an integral part of the curriculum.

- Staff Training: coordinate with the school librarian to assist in trainings that highlight services the public library offers that support the school library.

- Subscription Based Services: some examples include: foreign language programs, databases, eBooks, audiobooks, and homework help for students.

- Kits: education kits for primary grades that include books and props, CDs/DVDs, and so forth.

- Interlibrary Loan: while this is not technically a teacher-only resource, understanding how this process works at your library is essential for teachers, as some school districts do not have interlibrary loan policies.

Required Preparation: Complete volunteer applications and establish a relationship with the school librarian.

Additional Technology Requirements: none

Tips and Suggestions: During the first few weeks back to school, the principal typically must provide several hours of in-service for teachers. This is a great time to get your foot in the door at most schools. Another avenue for collaboration is working with the librarian by co-teaching a class that will earn the teachers professional development hours. In the spring, there are always teachers panicking because they don't have all their professional development hours. A class during this season may earn you the opportunity to speak with an audience that might surprise you. Professional development during the spring and early summer will introduce you to teachers who are focusing on helping students succeed both in the classroom and in academic testing. A second group of teachers represents those who have already started looking ahead to the next school year. Because time is limited, many teachers choose the summer to revise and enhance curriculum. Helping them see where the public library can help support the classroom is vital.

Worksheets/Rubrics: n/a

4

Starting off Simple:
LaterThis Tutorial

LaterThis is a very simple way of familiarizing yourself with the idea of bookmarking. What I enjoy most about LaterThis is it allows you time to think about what you will really use and what you won't. Sometimes when collecting resources, I get excited and mark everything, only to find out that the source isn't as credible as expected or had too many broken links. This can be frustrating if you use a lot of tagging when you bookmark as I do. LaterThis allows me to mark a site I'm interested in and come back later. This is particularly helpful when you take a tangent while researching. You might come across a great site that just isn't on that specific topic, but one you don't want to forget about.

Another benefit of LaterThis is that if you get interrupted frequently, or other people use your computer, you don't have to worry about your open tabs disappearing. Trust me—it's important. I worked for an hour finding resources once, all of which I had opened in tabs because I wanted to check for validity. Someone jumped on my computer while I was helping a student and then closed the browser after they were finished using my computer. ARG . . . LaterThis will prevent this from happening to you.

LaterThis and Delicious share information very easily. If bookmarking is new to you, get comfortable with the process of saving a bookmark and adding tabs, and then you can import from LaterThis into Delicious. Keep in mind though that LaterThis does not have the same networking component with peers. It is interactive in that you can share links, but you cannot browse through your peers' links at this time.

Step 1: Create an Account

Click **Create Your Free Account** and sign up. This does not require e-mail confirmation. LaterThis will leave you logged in for several days before it logs you out. If you share computers, log off when you are finished; if not it is more practical just to stay logged in to the site.

> **Create your free account**

Step 2: Add the Bookmarklets

Drag and drop the LaterThis and the LaterThis Quick icons to your toolbar, if desired. The first allows you to save and tag, and the second just quickly marks it for reference later. You will need to install these on any computer that you plan to use with LaterThis. These short cuts use pop-ups to install, so if you have these blocked, you may need to allow pop-ups for this site. You will know this applies to you if you see a flashing yellow bar giving you directions at the top of the browser. To allow pop-ups, click on the yellow bar and give the program permission.

> **LATERTHIS**
> - Opens in current browser window
> - Allows you to add comments and tags

> **LATERTHIS quick**
> - Opens in a popup
> - Saves a link with one click

Once you've installed these items, you can opt to hide this page of directions. It is best to hide the directions once you are comfortable with the website and have installed it on all your computers. → Don't show this page anymore

Step 3: Add Bookmarks

Typically with LaterThis, I bookmark as I'm looking at websites, not within the LaterThis site because it reduces the need to cut and paste. Find a website you are interested in and push the LaterThis Quick icon. This will place the bookmark in your unread links and you can go back and add it later. If you are not logged in to LaterThis, the prompt box will ask you to log in before it can add the link to your account. If you have difficulty, watch the tutorial on the welcome screen for more information. It goes through the process step by step and is very helpful.

I do not routinely use the full post a link icon because I haven't decided at that point if I want to keep the link, so I'd rather not devote the extra time to comments and tags. Plus, adding tags with only a cursory glance at the website might mean it gets tagged incorrectly, thereby becoming less valuable when searching for items by tag. For that reason, 90 percent of the time, I use the LaterThis Quick option.

Step 4: Manage Your Bookmarks

When you are ready to decide what to keep and what to discard in your bookmarks, log back into LaterThis. The tabs at the top of the screen are the navigation tool for bookmarking. Remember you can hide that welcome tab when you are finished or leave it for later reference.

Latest links: These are the bookmarks you've most recently added. This allows you to mark as read to show you've looked at it and want to keep it, delete, add to Delicious, or get more information from the URL. The feature used most in latest links is the edit feature. This is where you add any comments, tags, and mark bookmarks private, if applicable.

Edit link

Url

http://shackstacks.wikispaces.com/

Title

shackstacks - home

Comment (optional)

Tags (optional)

Separate with commas

☐ Private (only you can see this link)

Archive: Allows you to view all previous links.

Starred: Star those links you like the most.

Tags: View websites with the same tags. You cannot make changes here, only view the tags. This is where you will go when you want a link on a specific topic.

Step 5: Settings

Located in the top-right corner is the Setting button. Setting is where you go to change basic account settings. These include:

- E-mail
- Password
- Change if your added links are public or private
- Avatar
- Social Networking connections
- Exporting links

5

Practical Application: Putting LaterThis to Work

LaterThis is a little different than some of the other projects in the book, because it is primarily a tool for bookmarking sites for later review. Using LaterThis helps you to organize links. LaterThis will also allow multiple computers to be logged onto the same account, so when working with students, use a generic school account.

Personal Use

This will seem crazy, but bookmarking a site in a social bookmarking site is almost an emotional commitment to me. Individuals who share my links look at me as an authority, and if I've bookmarked and tagged a site, it is like putting my stamp of approval on that site. That is the allure of LaterThis. I can mark a site for review and then determine later whether I want to add to my permanent links. Another benefit of LaterThis is that I can be easily distracted when researching links. Rabbit chasing sometimes proves invaluable when I stumble across gems I'll use later, but using LaterThis keeps me from going too far off track.

Using LaterThis in an Academic Setting

Lesson/Activity: Name It to Play It

Common Core Standards: Research to Build and Present Knowledge.

Details: Students research and evaluate interactive websites and games and suggest them for inclusion on the library website. Websites must meet the requirements on Rubric 1 with a score of 3 or higher. If students search for websites at home, they will need to make sure the sites aren't blocked by the school filter. Allow students to nominate websites for two weeks and then have a special afterschool event where students use the computer to play these games.

Required Preparation: Establish an account for school-wide use. It should not contain any personal bookmarks or items you are worried about students deleting accidentally, or on purpose.

Additional Technology Requirements: none

Tips and Suggestions: Collect the top 10 websites from different subjects and forward to those teachers. Encourage them to suggest any additional websites. Once you have a good working list, use LiveBinders to create a list of great interactive, yet educational, websites.

Worksheets/Rubrics: Rubric 1: Interactive Website Recommendation.

Lesson/Activity: Online Dissection Websites

Common Core Standards: Key Idea and Detail 3.

Details: Science budgets and programs vary not only from district to district, but also from campus to campus. Provide a list of links for science teachers and students where virtual dissections can be utilized if funding makes actual dissections cost prohibitive. Also include dissections of things like owl pellets. Allow students and teachers to add suggestions, if possible.

Required Preparation: Locate and bookmark sites.

Additional Technology Requirements: Projector if using for whole-group instruction.

Tips and Suggestions: Be careful with young students to preview the content first. Some dissections are animation based, and some are designed for med students. Take a few minutes to preview the content to ensure that the dissection targets the appropriate audience.

Worksheets/Rubrics: n/a

Lesson/Activity: Student-Recommended Exercise Tutorials

Common Core Standards: n/a

Details: As a part of national student fitness week, encourage students as they locate websites that focus on different forms of exercise. Giving students time for thoughtful research allows them a chance for identification of an exercise or sport they might have been interested in but not know a lot about. If students locate games that can be used in Physical Education, be sure to share the list with the Phys Ed teachers.

Required Preparation: Create a general account.

Additional Technology Requirements: none

Tips and Suggestions: If you have after-school programs on your campus, share the bookmarks with the organizers as suggestion for activities to incorporate into their curriculum.

Worksheets/Rubrics: n/a

Lesson/Activity: Information about Weeding

Common Core Standards: n/a

Details: There is a plethora of information on weeding techniques on the Internet created by librarians. Weeding is a process that helps a librarian determine how to get rid of worn, outdated, or obsolete materials. Many school districts even have their weeding policies posted. Create a collection of these resources for reference before weeding. Becoming emotionally attached to your collection can mean more reticence when weeding because you have memories and experiences attached to particular resources. Review tips and suggestions before weeding. Create a Personal Learning Network with other librarians in your district by sharing and developing these resources together.

Required Preparation: Locate and bookmark websites.

Additional Technology Requirements: none

Tips and Suggestions: If your library budget is small, consider adding links with suggestions on growing your collection through fundraising, grants, donations, and so on.

Worksheets/Rubrics: n/a

Using LaterThis in a Public Library Setting

Service/Activity: Nominate a DVD

Community Connection: Schedule a DVD screening night in the community for a popular movie. The focus will depend on your audience. A family movie appeals to a broader base, but a movie that has a sequel releasing soon will earn the library a lot of free PR. The library or a small collaborative group should choose the first movie, to allow time for public performance right approval. Procuring public viewing rights is a must. Most movie companies will allow licensing of a video for a one-time performance, at minimal cost. Allow enough time between subsequent movie nominations and the movie show date for payment and paperwork. Coordinate with a local food bank or blood bank if your audience would participate in that kind of outreach.

Overview: Show a movie to get the community interested in the Nominate a DVD project. During the next four to six weeks, allocate a computer for patrons in a visible area of the library. Patrons will log in to LaterThis with the generic log in. LaterThis will remember the password for several days, unless logged out. Using a website like Internet Movie Database (IMBD) (/www.imdb.com/) patrons can bookmark movies they would like to see the library add to the collection. The winning video for the second video showing can either be the most popular video recommended or one chosen randomly from the recommended links; this will mainly depend on what you can get access to show. This video will only be shown after public performance rights have been acquired. Showing videos quarterly or twice a year allows for adequate time to secure permission. An added benefit from an activity like this is that patrons are making suggestions you can use when purchasing both books and movies because it will show you the most popular genres.

Required Preparation: Establish an account for library recommendations only. It should not contain any personal bookmarks.

Additional Technology Requirements: none

Tips and Suggestions: Add a link on the main website with directions for logging into LaterThis. Consider using the suggestions as an indicator for reading groups, clubs, and special events.

Worksheets/Rubrics: n/a

Service/Activity: List of Guest Speakers and Performers

Community Connection: n/a

Overview: As you develop a list of guest speakers and individuals who present at the library, use the star feature in LaterThis as a scoring tool. Consider the overall success of the event and the performance. In the comments section, make notes about cost for later reference or suggestions for better results in the future.

Required Preparation: Locate bookmarks for guest speakers and presenters.

Additional Technology Requirements: none

Tips and Suggestions: Be sure to mark these links private so that only you can see them, especially if you are adding comments about the event.

Worksheets/Rubrics: n/a

Service/Activity: List of Purchasing and Budgeting Tools

Community Connection: n/a

Overview: Create a login to share with local librarians in your city or county. Create a list of websites that simplify purchasing. These can include budgeting tools, book review websites, special discounts and offers, purchasing guidelines, highly circulating items, link to a Google document where community members suggest books, and so on.

Required Preparation: Creation of bookmarks and Google document if desired.

Additional Technology Requirements: none

Tips and Suggestions: Not all patrons will feel comfortable with Google documents. Have an offline suggestion area, as well.

Worksheets/Rubrics: n/a

6

Starting off Simple: Sqworl

Sqworl differs visually from other bookmarking sites we will cover in that it uses mini screen shots to create a visual link to a bookmark. This can be particularly helpful with certain populations. Those with limited English proficiency will appreciate recognizing the website from a picture rather than a name. Those individuals uncomfortable with technology will find the pictures more like locating facts in a book than trying to remember which tab to click, or which link provided the information they require. Visual learners also prefer Sqworl, because they know what the website looked like but don't always remember the name. In the mobile version of Sqworl there are no picture links, but the navigation is easy simple and easy to use, even on devices with small displays.

While a user ID is required to add links to a project, it is not required to access the project or search other collections of links. That means that, as a librarian, I can create a wealth of bookmarks for students to use in projects, and they only need the website address provided by Sqworl to view these sites.

Sqworl is a relatively new social networking tool, but it has gained more notice in the educational world over the past year. It will be interesting to follow the success of this tool over the next few years.

Step 1: Create an Account

This is simple and only requires a user ID and e-mail. Confirmation is not required, nor is your name. If you click on account after joining, you can opt out of e-mail updates if you aren't interested. Sqworl leaves you logged in, so if you share a computer, make sure to log off when you are finished using your account.

Step 2: Add the Bookmarklet

If you plan on using Sqworl regularly, I would add the bookmarklet to your desktop. Click on the image.

Browser Bookmarklet

Follow the directions to drag and drop the icon onto your toolbar

Sqworl Bookmarklet

The Sqworl Bookmarklet will allow you to add the URL you're currently viewing to one of your Sqworl groups without leaving the web page. You can even create a new group on the spot.

Drag **Add to Sqworl** to your toolbar.

Note: IE users should right click and select Add to Favorites

This is not required to use the website, but can be a timesaver if you plan on using the website for multiple projects. If you are going to simply be bookmarking specific sites into collections, this may not be a feature you need. If you add it and then change your mind later, you can always delete the site.

Step 3: Create a Group

A group on this website isn't a group of followers like you might think of on Twitter or Facebook. In Sqworl, a group is a collection of the websites you want to bookmark that are about a similar topic. Click on the group button and then name your group of bookmarks based on the content (science websites, Newbery Award authors, etc.). The description should be one to two sentences about the content being covered.

Once you create a group, Sqworl will provide you with a unique URL to share with others.

Done? Here is your public url: http://sqworl.com/jo98k0

Step 4: Add Websites

The next step is adding the websites. If you are not using the bookmarklet feature, then copy and paste the website into the URL box and provide a short description for users. This box can also contain notes if you need users to click on a particular part of the website. Click **Add**.

The picture may take a moment to show up, as the website has to do some behind-the-scenes formatting, but typically once you have the next bookmark in, the previous one will be complete. If no picture shows up, you might verify the link. That is one clue that your link wasn't copied correctly.

Under the picture, there is a tiny acorn and an automatically generated name of the creator of this website. If using a smart device to access Sqworl, make sure this title makes sense, as this is the text that displays in the list form. These can be very random, so use the edit function to change the title to text that makes sense to you.

Under the name of the link is a short description of the website. This is the text you added originally, but you can change this at any time. If doing an activity that has questions, you can even use the text to add directions or questions. If the content is under a subtab or requires opening a document, this is a good place to make notes for the end user.

If you are using the bookmarklet feature, when you are on the page you want to bookmark, click the bookmarklet and tell the program where to save. To me, this option is time consuming when I am only working on one group at a time. This becomes beneficial if you set up multiple groups and then plan on adding websites as you find them.

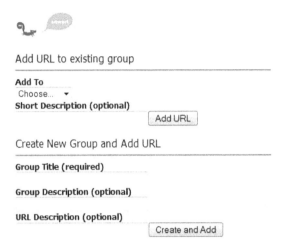

Step 5: Verify Your Links

When you are finished adding links, double check that you do not have duplicates (easy to do if you hit add twice or if you hit the refresh button for any reason). If you do, you can click the **x** in the corner to delete. Check for spelling mistakes or changes you would like to make. Here is a sample of a group with a few bookmarks to provide interactive math activities.

Math Links

pasadenaisd

Interactive lessons
by subject

shodor

Interactivate

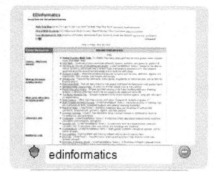

edinformatics

Collection of great
math sites

math-play

Math Games

homeschoolmath

Math activities with
a focus on home school

funbrain

Fun Brain for Junior
High Levels

update

awesomelibrary

Links from Awesome
Library-close top pop
up

aaamath

Math help grades K-8

Step 6: Group Information and Sharing

When you are finished, click your user ID at the top right corner to get back to your main page.

When you click on the mini graph, you will see any time someone has referred or tweeted about your group. The binoculars will let you get ideas from other groups with links similar to yours.

Leveled Book Database, Libraries, AR, OPAC, etc

for digital libraries

If you find a group that interests you, scroll down to the bottom of the page and click on the heart, and the group will be added as one you follow. You can also share the lists here.

Step 7: Sqworl Mobile

Sqworl does not have an app for use with smart phones; however, you can point your browser to the website (http://sqworl.com/m). Once you log on, you will see your groups in list form and then when you click on a group, you will see your links in list form. It does not provide pictures, but it is very easy to navigate. One feature to note is that the link titles come from the ones Sqworl names, so if they don't make sense to you when setting up your groups, you might want to rename these, in case people use the mobile site.

Directions are on the Sqworl blog or click on this link from your main page.

Sqworl Mobile

7

Practical Application:
Putting Sqworl to Work

While Sqworl does require an account ID to create content, it does not require an account to view content. In the search box, just type the content and any searchable list of links on that topic appears. The screen shot method of viewing these links is much less intimidating for individuals reluctant to use technology. Because fewer links are show on a page, this is helpful to younger children, when only a limited amount of links are needed, or when building a knowledge base for a new topic. The visual nature and easy searching take some of the intimidation out of searching with those who aren't familiar with bookmarking, or who are only used to using search engines.

Personal Use

Initially, I did not think that I would use Sqworl for personal use, but I was wrong. An additional benefit is how well Sqworl displays on my smartphone. The picture feature disappears and just displays my links in lists. As long as I've done the work on the front end, this feature makes locating my links very easy.

Using Sqworl in an Academic Setting

Lesson/Activity: Math Sqworl

Common Core Standards: Language Progressive Skills L4.1g.

Details: Because of the rather obscure nature of some of the words, math and science vocabulary continues to challenge our students. Those students who struggle with English as a second language have a particularly difficult time on standardized tests, due to the vocabulary in the questions. In order to support curriculum, use Sqworl to provide interactive websites for students or vocabulary-building websites. Students can compare the interactive websites to the content they are using in class. If you did the LaterThis activity, you will already have a collection of great websites. Another good interactive website is SAILOn (www.pasadenaisd.org/sailon/). Group these collected websites by mathematical theme. Students can work in stations, with station 1 looking up fun facts in the Guinness Book of Worlds Records related to math, station 2 researching on Sqworl, station 3 practicing math in small groups with the teacher, and station 4 watching short video clips illustrating math concepts. These clips can be from the Internet or from student projects.

Required Preparation: Collect Sqworl links, video clips, and nonfiction books relative to the scientific topic of study.

Additional Technology Requirements: Video clips and timer or link to timer website.

Tips and Suggestions: For the student requiring more extension, let them create their own lists and share with other students. Arrange the groups so that the small groups being tutored by the teacher have a quieter area in which to work.

Worksheets/Rubrics: n/a

Lesson/Activity: Student Mini Research

Common Core Standards: Integration of Knowledge and Ideas 8 and 9 and Research to Build and Present Knowledge 7–9.

Math Links

pasadenaisd

Interactive lessons
by subject

shodor

Interactivate

edinformatics

Collection of great
math sites

math-play

Math Games

homeschoolmath

Math activities with
a focus on home school

funbrain

Fun Brain for Junior
High Levels

update

awesomelibrary

Links from Awesome
Library-close top pop
up

aaamath

Math help grades K-8

Details: Review the concepts most frequently researched and prepare different lists of helpful sites for those recurring topics. This can be used both
inside and outside the library. Appeal to History teachers for historical
time periods they lack adequate information on and then help support their
classroom instruction. If your district provides online databases, be sure to

include these in the list. A great thing to consider for mini research is introductory information before novel units. Teachers want to provide the scaffolding of background knowledge, but don't always have time to collect the required information.

Required Preparation: Sqworl research links.

Additional Technology Requirements: none

Tips and Suggestions: As students begin researching, allow them to fill out the research feedback form. Give them the opportunity to suggest changes or additions to your current list of resources

Worksheets/Rubrics: Worksheet 3: Research Feedback.

Lesson/Activity: Science Sqworl

Common Core Standards: Integration of Knowledge and Ideas 8 and 9 and Research to Build and Present Knowledge 7–9.

Details: When I think about science, my mind instantly wanders to the Discovery Channel. I've watched things there I never thought I'd be interested in, because of the presentation. This is your chance to allow students the same opportunity. Working with the science department, choose topics that students typically have trouble mastering. Allow them to use video, images, and text to bring that science concept to life. Students then create 5–10 questions about their topic on notebook paper. Have a peer proofread their questions and then spot-check to avoid embarrassing mistakes when they share papers. During a subsequent library visit, students will work with a partner. Student 2 will use the links bookmarked previously in Sqworl by student 1 to answer all the questions submitted by student 1. After answering the questions, student 2 will evaluate student 1's research using the provided rubric.

Required Preparation: Create user IDs /passwords, unless allowing students to create their own.

Additional Technology Requirements: none

Tips and Suggestions: When students finalize this project, be sure to forward the best to your principal. You are directly supporting curriculum and connecting writing skills with science. Encourage students to come up with a Super Stumper question that they think the teacher won't be able to answer. If they succeed, give them extra bonus points.

Worksheets/Rubrics: Rubric 2: Science Scoring Rubric.

teachersdomain

Electric Girl

co

Learning Circuits

andythelwell

Blobz

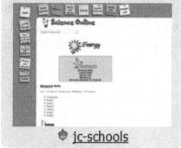

jc-schools

Science Online-Energy

missouri

ethemes

bnl

Both Magnetism and Electricity

hyperstaffs

Hyperstaff

sch

Science Zone

pppl

Ippex Online

howstuffworks

exploratorium

org

Lesson/Activity: Early Readers

Common Core Standards: Presentation of Knowledge and Ideas 5.

Details: As students begin to learn, it is important to expose them to many different sites to practice their letter recognition skills and beginning reading skills. Help overworked teachers by creating a list in Sqworl showcasing these websites. Collect books that do the same. These can be provided to the teacher to use in the classroom or used as a library lesson where students rotate from one station to the next. Station 1: books; Station 2: Sqworl;

Station 3: magazine station with old magazines where students can cut out images that start with a specific letter or the actual letter if they find it in text; Station 4: rhyming station that focuses on specific sounds. This can be poetry or simple tongue-twisters read aloud by the teacher or a volunteer and then taught to the student.

Required Preparation: Sqworl websites, pull books, find old magazines/construction paper, and collect rhyming poetry or tongue-twisters.

Additional Technology Requirements: none

Tips and Suggestions: With younger children, reviewing expectations before beginning is very important, as students should clearly understand what happens at each station so that they can begin working as soon as they arrive at that station. Using a timer helps keep everyone on track and allows enough time to review what students learned at each station before they leave the library.

Worksheets/Rubrics: n/a

Lesson/Activity: Famous Mathematicians

Common Core Standards: Social Studies Key Ideas and Details 1–3.

Details: Due to time constraints, mathematics focuses more on the math skill than on the individual who discovered the concept. Help teachers take a few minutes to study the mathematician behind the math by preparing links that focus on the founders of different mathematical concepts. These links can be grouped by either the person's name or the concept studied. Talk to the math teachers about what they would prefer.

Required Preparation: Locate and organize links in a Sqworl group.

Additional Technology Requirements: Projector, if viewing whole class.

Tips and Suggestions: Locate video clips when applicable, even if just a modern day recreation.

Worksheets/Rubrics: n/a

Lesson/Activity: Historical Figures

Common Core Standards: Integration of Knowledge and Ideas 8 and 9.

Details: Create Sqworl bookmark links containing biographical information on historical figures studied in particular sections of history. Teachers can use these for student projects or just as information to supplement the text. If possible, include timelines that show other events in history occurring during that person's life. Include information found in local databases so that teachers and students are familiar with what the databases have to offer. If databases require a user ID and/or password, make sure that students know where to get that information. Posting user IDs and passwords on the Internet is typically a violation of the licensing agreement, but directing them to the librarian for the password is not. Provide these passwords to students in a library brochure or database handout. If you have a computer lab in the library, post these logins directly on or near the computer.

Required Preparation: Locate and bookmark links.

Additional Technology Requirements: none

Tips and Suggestions: Remember to include links to the online catalog for books in your library collection.

Worksheets/Rubrics: n/a

Lesson/Activity: Architecture Styles

Common Core Standards: n/a

Details: Primarily for junior high and high school, links to the different types of architecture can be used not only in art but also in architecture classes. Many famous buildings have 3-D tours that clearly demonstrate the style, such as the Falling Water house designed by Frank Lloyd Wright (www.learn.columbia.edu/fallingwater/). Bookmark these sites as an overview of different types of architecture or create different lists with specific examples of that type of architecture.

Required Preparation: Locate and bookmark links.

Additional Technology Requirements: none

Tips and Suggestions: If possible, find links to examples within the community that students are familiar with seeing.

Worksheets/Rubrics: n/a

Lesson/Activity: Hands-On Crafts

Common Core Standards: n/a

Details: With school budgets facing drastic cuts, fine arts programs are suffering. Any support you can provide to art teachers will be greatly appreciated. Collect a list of websites that demonstrate hands-on crafts that can be incorporated into the art curriculum. Focus on projects that involve a minimal cost or which use recycled materials. If your art program has been reduced or eliminated, teachers will find these resources invaluable.

Required Preparation: Locate and bookmark websites.

Additional Technology Requirements: none

Tips and Suggestions: For older students, consider offering your art department books the next time you weed to use in found art projects. Students can take books and give them new life by turning them into an art project that incorporates both the old book and a new artistic interpretation.

Worksheets/Rubrics: n/a

Lesson/Activity: Home Management Tools

Common Core Standards: n/a

Details: If your campus has a life management class, help students by locating resources. These resources can include:

- How-to videos on dishwashing, doing laundry, simple home repairs, and so on

- Budgeting for the home

- Sewing tips and tricks
- Basic cooking tutorials or simply recipes
- Popular home remedies
- Green cleaning methods
- Recycling

Required Preparation: Locate and bookmark websites.

Additional Technology Requirements: none

Tips and Suggestions: Don't forget to show these websites both to students and teachers. The teachers may need the material you've bookmarked to supplement the curriculum content if it is too broad to reach the needs of all students.

Worksheets/Rubrics: n/a

Using Sqworl in a Public Library Setting

Service/Activity: Highlight Cookbooks and Local Restaurants

Community Connection: Supporting local businesses with free advertisement.

Overview: Hungry? Use Sqworl to showcase local restaurants or cooking websites. Try to include lesser-known but community-friendly restaurants as well as popular sites.

Have these available on a computer next to a cooking display of library books, or if that isn't possible, a print out of the links with information about how to access from home.

Required Preparation: Create a list of local restaurant websites as well as cooking tips websites and a display of cookbooks.

Additional Technology Requirements: none

Tips and Suggestions: Some patrons are afraid of cooking and some are chefs. If you have time create two different lists: one with family style restaurants and simple recipes, and the other with more complex recipes and upscale restaurants.

Worksheets/Rubrics: n/a

Service/Activity: Budgeting and Couponing Tips

Community Connection: Financial advisor on budgeting and or coupon lesson presenter.

Overview: With the recent downward trends in the economy, more and more patrons are struggling financially. What a perfect opportunity to show patrons your timeliness and resourcefulness. Arrange a special event with a financial advisor to speak on the importance of budgeting. Use Sqworl to provide links to sites that promote fiscal responsibility. Network with local parents in the community and find a couponing mom. Ask her to come present a workshop on how to coupon. Trust me—they love to share what they know. If possible, partner with a local food bank to discuss how couponing can allow you to support others in need. Provide handouts of Sqworl screenshots and links to websites that patrons can use at home to find the best deals.

Required Preparation: Arrange guests, bookmark Sqworl sites.

Additional Technology Requirements: none

Tips and Suggestions: Some local churches hold or offer money management or couponing classes. If you are having trouble locating someone to volunteer, they are a great resource.

Worksheets/Rubrics: n/a

Service/Activity: Websites for Home Projects

Community Connection: Mother's Day or Father's Day craft project involving stepping stones.

Overview: Homeowners are always looking for a way to make changes to their property without a lot of out-of-pocket expenses. Prior to Mother's Day or Father's Day, invite patrons to participate in a special creative project where they create stepping stones with handprints. While patrons are there, show give them a printout of Sqworl resources on other home improvement ideas. Also include links the Better Business Bureau (www.bbb.org/) and Angie's List (www.angieslist.com/) if they have a project to complete that requires outside help.

Required Preparation: Supplies for project and links for projects/resources.

Additional Technology Requirements: none

Tips and Suggestions: Local home improvement stores may be willing to donate supplies for free advertising.

Worksheets/Rubrics: n/a

Service/Activity: Information on Local Clubs for Children and Teens

Community Connection: Partnering with student programs.

Overview: There are many wonderful programs for young children and teens to get involved with during the year or during the summer. Some examples include Girl Scouts, Boy Scouts, Big Brother, Big Sister, 4-H, and so on. Coordinate with local representatives from these chapters and arrange a meet-and-greet where patrons can find out more about these events. Have bookmarks to these sites in Sqworl for additional information after the event is over.

Required Preparation: Arrange for meet-and-greet and bookmark websites.

Additional Technology Requirements: none

Tips and Suggestions: Don't forget to include local community organizations as well as national affiliations.

Worksheets/Rubrics: n/a

Service/Activity: Foreign Language Tutorials

Community Connection: n/a

Overview: These links can service both those trying to learn English as well as those trying to learn a different language. Using Sqworl, group interactive websites for language acquisition as well as links to local resources for language learning. If your library subscribes to a site like Mango Languages (www.mangolanguages.com/), use a program like Jing to capture step-by-step instructions for how to log on with a library username. Make sure not to show or say the actual password, but rather direct them to the librarian for that information.

Required Preparation: Locate bookmarks.

Additional Technology Requirements: none

Tips and Suggestions: If possible, have one list for each different language and possibly even one list for beginners, middle, and then advanced learners of each different language.

Worksheets/Rubrics: See the appendix for a tutorial on creating videos with Jing.

Service/Activity: The Power of Poetry

Community Connection: Mini writing workshop and Poetry Slam

Overview: My favorite celebration is Poetry month! Use Sqworl to promote sites where patrons can read poetry first. Then partner with a local writing group to do a mini workshop on writing poetry. Extend your Sqworl resources to include writing tips and tricks. Finally, use Sqworl to promote a celebration of poetry. Host a Poetry Slam, where patrons share original work. You can upload a video to YouTube (or another hosting site) and then post links on Sqworl.

Required Preparation: Sqworl sites, mini workshop presenter, and background information on Poetry Slams.

Additional Technology Requirements: none

Tips and Suggestions: If possible, set up one section of the library like a coffee house for the Poetry Slam. If budget allows buy small trophies for the winners.

Worksheets/Rubrics: n/a

8

Extending the Basics:
Jog the Web Tutorial

Jog the Web is a powerful tool for topical student research or providing information quickly for library patron access. With time at a premium, this site allows you to create a list of websites for quick access and text.

One downside to Jog the Web is that it uses frames, and some websites do not support frames. Responding to this concern, the creators have added an easy way to toggle into full screen mode. They have also added an error message that reduces the number of times students close Jog the Web unintentionally. In the free version, you cannot turn off comments, but it does notify you when a comment is added so you can delete, if necessary.

Step 1: Create an Account and Verify E-mail

Go to the Jog the Web website at http://jogtheweb.com. Click on the **register** button in the top corner.

This will require e-mail validation, so use an e-mail you can access easily. If you do not already have one, a Gmail account is a great place to create an e-mail to use for programs such as this. If you are at a school district, this will allow you easy access to verify e-mail, without worrying about the confirmations getting stuck in the spam filter.

Step 2: Create a New Jog

Click **create new Jog**.

Complete the information page and press **submit**. Both the title and description are visible by the public.

Step 3: Create a New Page

You have two choices when adding a new page. The first choice is to add a page on the Internet. The second is to add your own content. The latter is helpful for directions or as an introduction.

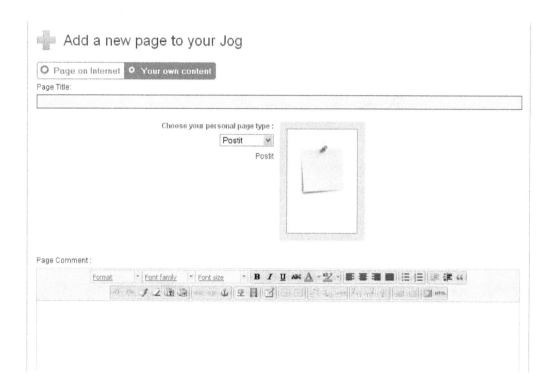

For this tutorial, we will begin with an introduction slide. Click on the **your own content** tab and then give the page a title. Using the drop box, you can change the type of page you create. Choose one that best matches your content or your audience.

Type your text below where it says page comment. You can format the page just as you would in any publishing program. Hover over a link to see what it does if you are unsure. When you are finished, click **save**. You do not want to click **I'm done editing** yet. That is what you click when you are finished with the entire jog. The page list now appears at the top.

Page 1

Introduction <u>Edit</u>

http://www.jogtheweb.com/step/1170130

If you notice it says your page title, that means you forgot to name the page. Click on **edit** to make that change and add text. This is important to the end user, so they know what link they are about to click (e.g., introduction, welcome, step 1, etc.).

From here, you can easily add pages, move pages up or down, or delete entire pages. The specific link to each page is also visible. A unique page is created for every page of original content.

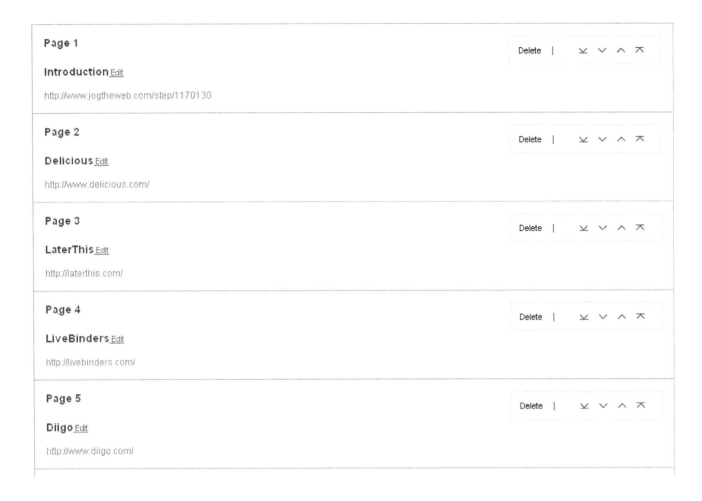

Now we will add a link by clicking **page on the Internet** rather than your own content. This option moves further and further down the page, depending on how many websites and offline pages you've added.

When you click **page on the Internet**, you only have to complete the title and the website. Use the comment field if you desire, but it is not required.

Continue adding websites or pages until you've included all the necessary websites. When you are happy with the order and the websites, go to the next step.

Step 4: Complete Your Editing

You will notice there is a link for when you are finished editing and also a link for properties. With the free version of Jog the Web, your options are very limited.

Once you hit **I'm Done Editing**, the jog will appear on your My Jog page.

On the back bar, you will notice three options. The first is to edit the jog. Use this to make any changes to your jog, following the steps above.

The second option is to share the jog. Use this link to get to provide the direct link to your jog.

The third option allows you to delete the jog entirely. Don't forget that if you delete a jog, you will need to remove it from anywhere that you embedded the code or you will get an error message on those websites.

Under the black bar, you can see how many views your jog has had as well as the index and jog it links. Index takes you to a list of the pages and websites on your jog. The jog it link will take you directly into the jog.

If you are logged in with your account, you can edit while in this view as well as add comments or post on various social networking sites. Other individuals will have all the same options, except for the editing rights.

Step 5: Using Jog the Web

Once inside the actual jog, the help features show up if you hover over any icon that has more information available. Options most used:

• Use the blue arrows to advance to the next page or click on the links on the left. You may need to explicitly teach this, as people are used to tabs on the top.

• Click on the creator to learn more about them or view other jogs they've created.

• Add a comment.

• If you are logged in, you can view the edit page option. Other individuals will not have that same option.

• When viewing a page, if the frame makes the website too small to view clearly, hold down **control** on the keyboard and click where it says **show page** URL to open up a separate window with that website. Sometimes sites that require a password will not work with frames. When the user is finished, they can close the window and they will be back at the Jog the Web.

• Share on social networks like Twitter and Facebook.

9

Practical Application: Putting Jog the Web to Work

One benefit of using Jog the Web with the public is that you get a very professional looking place for organizing bookmarks and adding text, without a lot of extra work. The blog at http://blog.jogtheweb.com/ is very helpful and questions are answered in a timely manner. Some of the auxiliary links on the website go bad from time to time, but overall the integrity of the site and its ease of use make it an invaluable tool. Jog the Web is an evolving tool and so, as with any growing entity, there have been a few growing pains. One of the benefits of Jog the Web is that the usage base is more international than some of the other sites.

Personal Use

The nature of Jog the Web makes it more for student and patron use rather than personal use, because you can only have private jogs at the subscription level. Personally, I like to have that administrative control, so while I do use Jog the Web quite frequently to share links/text, I do not use it for my personal links. The inability to turn off comments can also be an issue, depending on your audience.

Using in an Academic Setting

Lesson/Activity: Website Evaluation

Common Core Standards: Integration of Knowledge and Ideas 8 and 9 and Research to Build and Present Knowledge 7–9.

Details: One of the things that students struggle with most is how to tell if a website is an accurate or dependable website for research. Jog the Web allows you to create a step-by-step approach to help students come to their own decision about just using Google, alternative search engines like Sweet Search (www.sweetsearch.com/), or using an online database.

The first step would be to collect a group of websites that you know to be fake websites. Try to find some that are very clearly ridiculous and some that are so tricky they almost had you thinking they were real. Have these hoax websites listed first and then reveal in a text page the answers to which pages are real and which are fake. Discuss with students where to locate the misinformation on each website and how to determine the validity of a website. Provide them a rubric to use to evaluate websites as they begin their own research. Kathy Schrock has a step-by-step evaluation tool (http://school.discoveryeducation.com/schrockguide/eval.html). This is the perfect opportunity for students to recognize the value of online databases.

Required Preparation: Create a jog or locate one already created.

Website Validity		21 Steps
Edit Jog	Share	Delete

A step by stop jog to help discover the importance of knowing where your information comes from.

By : vandenbroek   **171 Views**   Index   Jog it

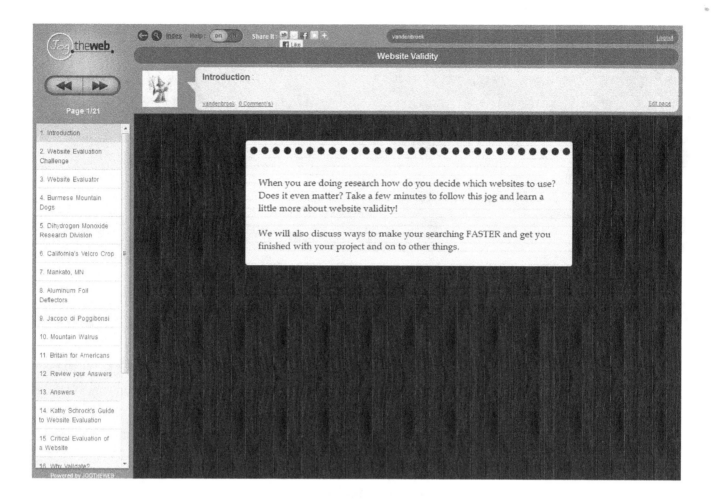

Additional Technology Requirements: None, unless combining with QR codes.

Tips and Suggestions: See suggestion in the QR code section for a way to incorporate both Jog the Web and QR codes.

Worksheets/Rubrics: n/a

Lesson/Activity: Book Trailer Tutorial

Common Core Standards: Key Ideas and Details 2.

Details: A digital book trailer is a commercial for books, similar to a movie trailer. Creating a Jog the Web for creating book trailers is a way to involve students, teachers, and administrators. First, create a Jog that details how to create a book trailer, with links to sites that make this more accessible. Here are a few examples:

- For creating the trailer (http://animoto.com or http://photopeach.com)

- For free photos (http://flickr.com/creativecommons), (http://morgue file.com), or (http://pics4learning.com).

- For photo editing (http://pixenate.com/).

- Examples of book trailers: (http://booktrailersforall.com/), (http://digitalbooktalk.com/), or (www.homepages.dsu.edu/mgeary/booktrailers/). Don't forget to showcase any book trailers you've created.

Here is a sample of an introductory page:

Want to Create Your Own Book Trailer?

Here are some overall steps for book trailers. Each book trailer website requires slightly procedures, but this will get you started. As I create handouts for the different websites and programs I'll add to the end of this jog.

Step 1: Brainstorm a list of about 10-15 pictures that tell the story of your book without giving away the ending. Remember that you won't be able to use copyrighted photos (like a photo from a movie). Be willing to change your mind because sometimes you can't find the exact photo you want. The school filter will not allow you to Google search for images, so we have some other options below.

Step 2: Log into the computer as you. Create a folder on the desktop with your name on it. You will save all photos/music into this file. Be sure to put this in your home folder at the end of the class period so you don't lose your work.

Required Preparation: Create or locate Jog the Web on creating a book trailer.

Additional Technology Requirements: If students are using computers at school, access to storage space like a server is helpful.

Tips and Suggestions: Once individuals feel comfortable with the process, begin to post their work on the library website. There is a sample permission form in the Worksheets section.

Worksheets/Rubrics: Worksheet 7: Permission Slip.

Lesson/Activity: Citation 101

Common Core Standards: n/a

Details: Another source of struggle for students is citing information in the correct format. While a majority of schools use MLA, the method of choice at colleges and universities depends largely on the area of study. Secondary librarians and colleges can help students by providing links to the most current citation information, tips on creating works cited, bibliographies, and in-text citations.

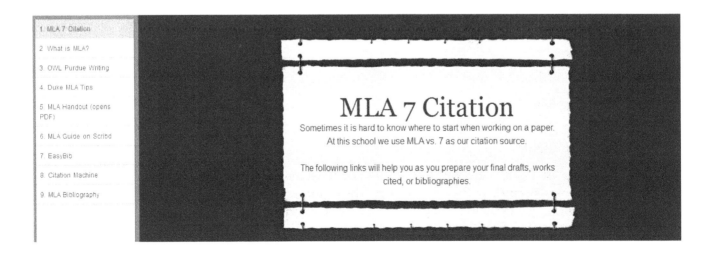

1. MLA 7 Citation
2. What is MLA?
3. OWL Purdue Writing
4. Duke MLA Tips
5. MLA Handout (opens PDF)
6. MLA Guide on Scribd
7. EasyBib
8. Citation Machine
9. MLA Bibliography

MLA 7 Citation

Sometimes it is hard to know where to start when working on a paper. At this school we use MLA vs. 7 as our citation source.

The following links will help you as you prepare your final drafts, works cited, or bibliographies.

Showcasing sites like EasyBib (http://easybib.com) is very beneficial for students. See the tutorial in the introduction section for more information.

Required Preparation: Create or locate Jog the Web on citation.

Additional Technology Requirements: none

Tips and Suggestions: Creating these tutorials may require an initial investment of time. If you are on a campus that uses more than just one citation style, try to collaborate with another colleague to divide the workload.

Worksheets/Rubrics: n/a

Lesson/Activity: Parts of a Book

Common Core Standards: Craft and Structure 5.

Details: Younger children need the help developing the vocabulary terms that represent the different parts of a book. This is especially true in families where not much reading occurs in the home. Create a Jog the Web that has text and pictures to focus on the different parts of a book. Bookmark websites that talk about those parts of the book. As a class, use a projector and computer to discuss these links. Discuss any library-specific labeling or identification that is important to students.

Place piles of different types of books on the middle of each table. Have students race to find the part discussed on their book. Students shouldn't use the same book more than two times in a row, so that they have exposure to what the parts of a book look like on a variety of different sizes, genres, and so on.

Required Preparation: Jog the Web with parts of a book images and links, pull a variety of different books (one for each child).

Additional Technology Requirements: Projector.

Tips and Suggestions: n/a

Worksheets/Rubrics: n/a

Lesson/Activity: Parent Resources

Common Core Standards: n/a

Details: At an elementary level particularly, a librarian can be a great advocate for parents. While some parents are reluctant to get involved with school due to previous experience, a librarian is typically a safe way to get involved. Support parents using Jog the Web by providing resources on helping their student have a successful school experience. Make sure to watch the reading level on the articles you bookmark. Articles that are too collegiate may intimidate parents rather than support them. Some examples of topics to include:

- Immunization information. Consult your school nurse for the best resources.
- Information about the hidden rules of school. Parents who had bad experience in school may just not have understood some of the school's social norms or classroom expectations.
- Local free and fun activities for students.

- Opportunities for parents to volunteer at school and in the library.

- How to help children with homework.

- Events and services at the public library.

- Tips for reading with children.

- Links to websites that have eBooks or audio books for free.

- Tips for dealing with parenting issues such as anger management, strong-willed children, shyness, and so on.

Required Preparation: Bookmark websites and then promote with parents.

Additional Technology Requirements: n/a

Tips and Suggestions: If your school sponsors a reading night for the entire campus, this would be a perfect opportunity to discuss the resources the library can provide parents.

Worksheets/Rubrics: n/a

Lesson/Activity: Mathematical Discoveries

Common Core Standards: Social Studies Key Ideas and Details 1–3.

Details: Have students log into their own Jog the Web account and create an overview of a mathematic discovery that they find interesting. The jog should include background information, who was involved in the discovery, why it impacted mathematics, and how it personally relates to the student.

Required Preparation: Have a list of mathematical discoveries that is appropriate to the grade level. Help students set up individual Jog the Web accounts.

Additional Technology Requirements: Projector for in-class use.

Tips and Suggestions: When research is completed, the teacher can use the jogs in the classroom as filler at the start or end of class, or before introducing one of the researched topics.

Worksheets/Rubrics: Rubric 3: Mathematical Discovery.

Lesson/Activity: Anger Management

Common Core Standards: n/a

Details: One way of reducing the number of visits to the office for behavioral reasons is education. Students need to learn ways of managing their anger and frustration in an academic setting. The increasing lack of anger management skills is clear from elementary through college age students. It is critical that we as educators equip students with the ability to understand and control their anger. Students must understand what triggers their anger and how to handle it in a way that is appropriate for school. Create a list of resources for students. If your campus has a study hall or advisory period, provide this list of resources to teachers as a tool for direct instruction or reinforcement if anger is a behavior causing trouble for a particular student.

Required Preparation: Locate and create a jog with links and text to support anger management skills. Text and links should be appropriate for the audience. Order links using a sequential sorting hierarchy so that the skills and topics build. These topics can include:

- How to tell when you are angry.

- What triggers your anger.

- How to control your anger.

- Specific tips for managing anger in schools.

- Why anger management is important.

- How trouble with anger affects relationships.

- Games that review concepts.

- Helpful links for more information.

Additional Technology Requirements: none

Tips and Suggestions: Coordinate with the counselors to add any text in support of the located links. Three good websites include Angries Out (www.angriesout.com/), Kids Health (http://kidshealth.org/teen/), and the APA (www.apa.org).

Worksheets/Rubrics: n/a

Lesson/Activity: Anti-Bullying Resources

Common Core Standards: n/a

Details: Another social component easily highlighted with Jog the Web is bullying. Collect resources that identify what is bullying and what is not. Use the user-created page as a tool for student who are struggling with bullying or who aren't sure how to report it to school administration. Provide explicit instruction for each group: bullies, those being bullies, and those who know someone who fits those descriptions.

Required Preparation: Locate and bookmark links and add support text.

Additional Technology Requirements: none

Tips and Suggestions: Don't forget to include cyber bullying, because although that typically occurs outside of school, the fallout carries over into school.

Worksheets/Rubrics: n/a

Lesson/Activity: Background Information on Artists

Common Core Standards: Integration and Knowledge 7–9.

Details: Create a Jog the Web for a variety of different popular artists. Think of this as a virtual portfolio of the artist. Include:

- Biographical information from childhood through adulthood.
- Random and interesting facts.

- Information about the styles/medium of choice.

- Websites.

- Samples of their work.

- If still living, information about current art shows.

- Links to library resources on this artist or their style.

- Art tips for creating a similar work or style.

Required Preparation: Locate and bookmark links.

Additional Technology Requirements: none

Tips and Suggestions: Coordinate with a high school art teacher for this project. Sometimes, upper-level classes require a student research project and students may be willing to share research project with you. With student permission, upload their finished projects to a site like Vuzit (www.vuzit.com/), which will allow you to embed the document and provide you a link to include in your jog so that students can have a sample. To reduce the temptation for plagiarism, rotate the samples so that the ones displayed are not researched that grading period.

Worksheets/Rubrics: n/a

Lesson/Activity: Research a Historical Time Period

Common Core Standards: Integration of Knowledge and Ideas 7–9 and Research to Build and Present Knowledge 7–9.

Details: Use Jog the Web to focus on specific time periods. Initially, create one Jog the Web to show the History/Social Studies Department the concept. If popular, allow students to create their own Jog the Web for a unit being covered in class and compare as a class. Present a variety of topics for a well-rounded look at the time period:

- Important people.

- Scientific discoveries.

- Everyday life.

- Historical events.

- Popular music or culture.

- Fun facts.

- Literature.

- Relevant pictures and video.

- Timeline.

Required Preparation: Create an initial Jog the Web for a time period covered in the History/Social Studies curriculum. Prepare enough in advance that this can be used in instruction. If they exist, use links contained in any curriculum documents. This initial jog serves not only as a teaching tool for the classroom teacher, but also as an example of your expectations for finished student projects.

Additional Technology Requirements: Projector for classroom use.

Tips and Suggestions: Look at previous standardized test scores, if applicable, and choose an area of focus that traditionally has lower test scores.

Worksheets/Rubrics: n/a

Lesson/Activity: Hidden Academic Rules and Norms

Common Core Standards: n/a

Details: This activity is geared toward first-generation college-bound students or students who had parents that dropped out of school. A majority of these students do not have the prior background knowledge to understand the ins and outs of academia. Directly teaching students these skills helps them understand why a rule exists rather than just requiring them to follow it because they are told to do so. This jog will require a significant amount of user-created text. Find a website that demonstrates the hidden rule and then discuss in user-created text what that looks like on your campus. Allow students to use the comment feature to ask questions or add comments. Some examples of topics include:

- How to address teachers in the hallway who aren't your teacher.

- How to create a homework station at home.

- Organizational skills.

- Note-taking.

- Handling peer pressure.

- Home rules vs. school rules.

- When to ask for help.

- Why standardized tests are important (also included are advanced placement tests and college entrance tests).

- Time management.

- Dealing with people you don't like.

Required Preparation: Significant amount of user-created text to supplement links.

Additional Technology Requirements: Projector, if used in the classroom.

Tips and Suggestions: At the end of the year, survey first-year junior high, high school, and college students for a hit list of the things that they felt the most unprepared for that year. Make sure those are covered in your discussion topics.

Worksheets/Rubrics: n/a

Use in a Public Library Setting

Service/Activity: Genealogy Resources

Community Connection: Local members of the community who are researching lineage.

Overview: Depending on your collections, genealogy resources and books might be very important to your community. As professional guidance is not always available to help these patrons search their family histories, providing helpful guidance in the form of Jog the Web can be invaluable.

Create the jog using help from experts and community members who have had success researching their lineage. Host a brainstorm session and add suggestions in real time. Use their practical expertise to help establish best practices and most useful websites.

Required Preparation: Flyer to advertise brainstorm event, Jog the Web to store links and text.

Additional Technology Requirements: none

Tips and Suggestions: If technology allows, have these jogs available in the genealogy section on computers dedicated to researching genealogy.

Worksheets/Rubrics: n/a

Service/Activity: Highlight Community Events

Community Connection: none

Overview: Most towns have a variety of community events to highlight. On your website, post a Jog the Web with connections to websites that promote local theater, kid-friendly events, music events, or chances to volunteer in the community. Include direct links to calendars on local community pages or have a community volunteer add text Jog the Web pages that include important events. If you don't have a community volunteer already, look at retired individuals who spend a lot of time in the library and ask them to help with this community outreach. Post a suggestion box in the library where patrons can add suggestions of events to add to the jog. Look for individuals making good suggestions as a potential source for a new volunteer partnership.

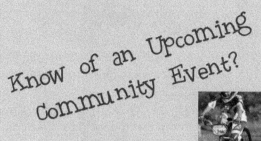
Know of an Upcoming Community Event?

Drop off an event form or see a librarian to have the event considered for addition to the Community Events Listing.

Required Preparation: Organize a list of community events and suggestion box.

Additional Technology Requirements: none

Tips and Suggestions: Contact the local theaters, concert halls, and so forth, for a listing of upcoming events. Another useful source is the local Parent Teacher Association president. You can speak with the PTA president and ask to be included on newsletters or upcoming event e-mails. These events can be added in a text page. Additionally, the PTA president can provide contact with other volunteers who also serve on community committees. These individuals will come from a variety of backgrounds and may know about some lesser-known events and be willing to include you on their update lists.

Worksheets/Rubrics: Worksheet 4: Community Event Suggestion.

Service/Activity: Applying for Scholarships & College Entrance Tests

Community Connection: Connections between high schools/colleges and public libraries.

Overview: Students aren't always aware that the public library has a wealth of information on earning college scholarships or taking college exams. Most libraries have study guides for the major exams in both their reference and nonfiction sections. School districts try to keep students informed, but many students do not get the funds or support they need to be successful simply because they do not know those resources are available. Differentiate your Internet and book resources clearly so that patrons will know the library supports both first-time college students, returning college students, and upper-level college students.

Required Preparation: Locate and bookmark links. Create tutorial slides with step-by-step instructions.

Additional Technology Requirements: none

Tips and Suggestions: College students frequently earn substantial library fines because they keep books for a class or simply forget to turn them back into the library. Allow students who successfully pass a test or earn a scholarship to complete a jog with their newly acquired information. After students share their jog with the library, waive some or all of the student's library fines.

Worksheets/Rubrics: n/a

Service/Activity: Creating a Resume

Community Connection: Resume 101 workshop.

Overview: Ask a local business figure to speak to patrons on the topic of resumes. Highlight the dos and don'ts of good resume writing and what they look for when choosing a candidate to interview. Publicize the event in advance and provide links to patrons that include tutorials on resume creation, good and bad examples, tip and tricks, and, if appropriate, resume templates. Encourage attendees to bring their resume for informal evaluation and feedback. Provide workspaces for patrons to make revisions to their resume.

Required Preparation: Arrange guest speaker and locate and bookmark links.

Additional Technology Requirements: Projector and document camera for presentation.

Tips and Suggestions: Local unions are one source of information, as well as the Chamber of Commerce. If possible, invite local businesses who are hiring. They can help critique resumes but may find a new employee in the process. If budget allows purchase, or have donated, mini USBs to store the patrons' resume. A 2GB or smaller USB can be purchased very inexpensively.

Worksheets/Rubrics: n/a

Service/Activity: Teen Manga Club

Community Connection: Highlight local Manga club.

Overview: If you create a generic login for Jog the Web, club members can access a page and make additions and changes. The comments portion of Jog the Web is a great way to share opinions on links or ideas. For a Manga club, focus on websites that introduce Manga, links to popular Manga sites, book reviews on Manga, and even writing and illustration tips for creating their own Manga. If desired, participants can create their own works and post. Jog the Web will not let you upload handouts, but they can be posted on your server with a link or on another Cloud-based hosting site.

Required Preparation: Jog the Web structure with some initial information.

Additional Technology Requirements: none

Tips and Suggestions: Keep in mind that if patrons plan to publish their work, posting on the Internet could be a mixed blessing. It might get their work exposure, but it might make it too available to the public.

Worksheets/Rubrics: n/a

Service/Activity: Crisis Tools and Tricks

Community Connection: Fire department visit to the library.

Overview: If you live in an area prone to natural disasters, such as tornadoes, floods, and earthquakes, helping patrons be prepared can reduce the scope of disaster. Sites like http://ready.gov help review what individuals need in case of an emergency. If the event is planned on a Saturday, coordinate with local fire department or hospitals for volunteers, because nothing draws a crowd of parents like a fire truck.

Use Jog the Web to bookmark important sites and use the text feature to add information that is specific to your community. Be sure to include the emergency directions for the library. Provide this information to attendees and showcase how patrons can use computers in the library at no charge. This is often a service that not all community members are aware of, so it's a great chance to get the full spectrum of library services out to the public.

Required Preparation: Arrange for donations, bookmark sites, contact fire department.

Additional Technology Requirements: n/a

Tips and Suggestions: If you are going to promote an emergency bag, ask a local business to donate the bags for anyone who attends the workshop. The emergency bag can include suggestions of what the patron should store in the bag at home in case of an emergency. A complete list is available at the Ready.gov website, and includes things like water, snacks, first aid kits, flashlights, and other supplies that might be needed, depending on the region in which you live. Local businesses are typically eager to donate, because it is a great way for them to get free advertising if they choose to purchase bags with their logo.

Worksheets/Rubrics: n/a

10

Extending the Basics: LiveBinders Tutorial

When you think about LiveBinders, think about Jog the Web but on collaboration steroids. In Jog the Web, only one person can edit a jog at the same time. This is perfect if you only need to reference a few websites, you have the time to create the content, or if sequential step-by-step research is important. If, however, you need to share multiple websites that fall into different categories, then LiveBinders is the best choice.

Think about LiveBinders like an old-school file folder keeping track of your links. You can have one page that has multiple websites on the same topic and then other pages with different topics. For example, students in my library were recently reading *A Wrinkle in Time*. Before they began the novel unit, they used LiveBinders to research the author, the topic of black holes, complete WebQuests related to prior knowledge, and then had a resource for help as they read the novel.

Before you get started, look at the binder page About Binders. It has some great resources for helping you create binders and maximize the collaborative portion of the website.

Step 1: Register for an Account

This site does require e-mail to register, but it does not require e-mail confirmation. Note, you have to be 13 or older to join, so this may be an issue if you are planning to have younger patrons complete their own LiveBinders. Anyone can use Live-Binders without being a member. You only need to be a member to edit.

Sign Up | Log In | Help

When you log in, you see tabs for account management in LiveBinders.

- **My Binders**: this tab is where all your binders are located. This is where you can edit or access your binder options.

- **Featured**: this tab shows different binders that they are highlighting that month. These are easily sorted by amount of views, categories, or creation date.

- **Learn More**: click here to start a new binder. Easy access to tutorials, webinars, and the LiveBinders blog. This is where you should go if you need any help creating or managing your binder.

- **Upgrade**: select if you want to upgrade to allow for more file size on uploads and total storage space. The free version is very robust so this may not be necessary depending on your needs.

- **Tools**: information on the LiveBinder It Tool, apps, and shelves. If you are using LiveBinders regularly, you may want to consider adding the short cut for the LiveBinders Bookmarklet tool. I usually create LiveBinders with a research focus and found that I didn't use the tool as much as I thought, and

80 Bookmarking

it was extra clutter on my browser I didn't need. Once you've been using LiveBinders for a while, you will know if the bookmarklet tool meets your need or not. The apps are powerful and the shelf allows for easy embedding into websites.

In addition to these tabs at the top of the LiveBinders website is a filter that allows you to search featured binders, your binders, educational binders, or search by creator.

Step 2: Create a Binder

Click on **Start a Blank Binder.**

Complete the blank binder description. I usually leave mine private as I'm working on it and then change to public once it's complete. Of course, I tend to work on projects in the few spare stolen moments I have, so it might take me a few days to build a binder. If you have a chunk of time to devote, you can set to public at the start.

Create New Binder

Please name your binder here:

Description:

Tags (comma separated):

Category: Personal ▾

○ **Public** - Everyone can view your binder
◉ **Private** - Only you, and the people you choose, can view your binder

Access Key - give this key to people when sharing this private binder:

Use Google search to fill a binder ○ Yes ○ No

* required

[Create New Binder]

On this screen, you can also provide an access key. Your site might be public so you can embed and others can easily view, but an access key gives you control over who views it. You must have an access key if the binder is set to private. This is particularly useful if student or patron work is displayed.

The Google search option allows you to fill automatically from Google using search words. This option creates a separate tab for each website. As you would expect, depending on your key words, this can be helpful or a waste of time. I prefer to set this to **no**.

Step 3: Binder Tabs

When you create a binder, you get three tabs to start. You can add or delete these tags as desired.

The active tab is always a different color from the other tabs.

Name the tab. The first tab is typically named the home tab or welcome tab. Click **one time** in the box, type the name of the tab, and then click on the next tab. The triangle on the tab allows you to move the tab, delete the tag, or add new subtags. This is where the lingo can get a little confusing. Remember that tabs have multiple uses.

1. A tab can be used as a homepage or as text with directions for an activity.

2. Tabs can showcase only one website. In this case, the name of the tag would typically be the name of the website.

3. A tab can incorporate a link to an image or document.

4. A tab can act as a file folder and contain subtabs of links to websites on a topic. For example, a tab might say Helpful Tax Resources and have links to several websites patrons would find beneficial when filing taxes.

5. If you create a video in Jing, you can insert that URL and the video will appear in the frame. That doesn't work with YouTube; those have to be added as media (see below).

Another way to add content is the **Enter a URL** button on each tab.

Enter a URL: [_____] [Insert] [New Tab] [New Subtab] [Go to Site]

Remember that tabs are the things at the top that actually look like old school binder tabs at the top of your binder. A subtab is the link that displays on that tab. As long as you the differentiation between tab and subtab in your mind you can add links in whatever way makes the most sense for you. You are probably going to mess this up at least once, so be patient. It took me a couple of accidental deletions before getting it straight. **Undo** is your best friend, but it is invisible unless you are in the editing mode. Step 4 shows several ways to add content.

Step 4: Editing Options

Click on the **edit menu** button. It will open up a series of options relating to files, tabs, media, text, and overall binder properties.

[Edit Menu]

Note that to close this window, you have to close it. Clicking tabs will not close the editor.

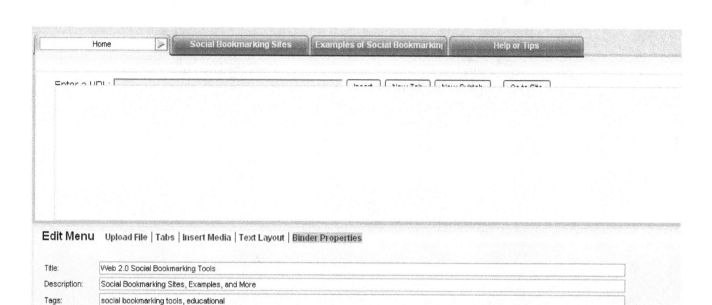

Upload File

This is where you can incorporate pictures, documents, files, and movies into a tab or subtab. Find the file on your computer and upload as desired. If you are uploading as a subtab, make sure you are on the tab where you want the document to appear. For a title, you can upload a PowerPoint slide saved as a jpeg.

Tabs

In addition to editing tabs at the top as discussed earlier, you can also edit tabs here. This also another place you can work with subtabs. Remember, the little box by the

triangle is the title of the site, tab, or subtab; the URL of the website goes below in the URL window.

Link for text.
Link for website.

Insert Media

Insert content from Flickr, YouTube, Delicious, or content in previously created binders.

Text Layout

This is the best way to format how text or images appear on a tab. This is particularly helpful when giving directions, overviews to the binder, or adding a table.

Binder Properties

Use this area to change the overall properties of your binder. You can change color here, switch from private to public, change the binder thumbnail, and so on.

| Edit Menu | Upload File | Tabs | Insert Media | Text Layout | Binder Properties |

Title:	Web 2.0 Social Bookmarking Tools
Description:	Social Bookmarking Sites, Examples, and More
Tags:	social bookmarking tools, educational
Category:	Education	Binder Author Name:
Access:	Private - Copy Disabled	Color: Green
Key:		Update

Undo

Hiding toward the right is your best friend, **undo**. If you get rid of a tab when you meant to delete a subtab, or vice versa, just click **undo** to restore. Whew!

Step 5: Sharing the Binders

When the binder is complete, you can share the link or embed the binder in your website. From the My Binders tab, use the drop-down **options** button to get the embed code. There are also several other options for posting on social networking sites, adding to shelves or sharing the link.

Name:	Web 2.0 Social Bookmarking ...
URL:	http://livebinders.com/play
Embed:	<div style="width:75px; he

You can embed a binder icon and link to a binder in your MySpace page or on any web page.

Simply copy the 'Embed' text above and paste it into your web page.

One feature I really like about LiveBinders is that it can be collaborative. Anyone who has a LiveBinders account can work with you on a binder if you choose to collaborate. From the My Binder tab, find the binder you want to share.

If you select **collaborate**, you can give rights to edit this binder to anyone with a LiveBinders account. You only need to know the e-mail they used to set up their account.

Email this LiveBinder
Collaborate
Show Details
Embed
Make a Copy
Edit It
Present
Delete It X
[Close]

When individuals are viewing your completed binder, the websites may not be optimally viewed in the LiveBinders boxes. If that is the case, they can go directly to the website by clicking the **go to site** option. Then they will typically close a tab

[Go to Site]

or window to return to the binder. Some people prefer to use tabs and others prefer new windows. You can change these settings at any time:

- In Firefox, choose **Options**, then **Tabs**.

- In Internet Explorer, choose **Tools** and then **Internet Options.**

- In Safari, choose **Edit**, then **Preferences**, then **Tabs**.

Step 6: Shelves

LiveBinders also allows you to group related binders into shelves you create. You can showcase all your binders on the same shelf or use shelves to reflect different topics. For example, you might create one shelf for science resources and one shelf for language arts resources. If you prefer, you do not have to use a shelf.

11

Practical Application: Putting LiveBinders to Work

Even if you never take time to create a LiveBinders account, spend time looking at the binders that have already been created. My guess is that you will be hooked. The quality varies, depending on who creates the binder, but rarely have I been disappointed with what is available and ready for use. Students and teachers benefit greatly from understanding the ease of searching already created binders without needing an understanding of how to create their own binders. Those familiar with LibGuides, a subscription product, will see many similarities that allow you to create your own free virtual library.

LiveBinders is different from some of the other social bookmarking tools in that it allows multiple users to work on the same binder. The only thing that is required is that the individuals have their own account. Once the initial binder is created, click on the options drop-down menu on the My Binders tab. Choose **collaborate** and then invite as many other members as desired.

Email this LiveBinder

Collaborate

Show Details

Embed

Make a Copy

Edit It

Present

Delete It ✗

[Close]

Personal Use

The search tool in LiveBinders is very robust! When looking for websites or ideas on a topic, LiveBinders is frequently the first place I go, because of the success I've had with the content and resources. Many teachers and librarians already use binders and some enable the share feature, which means I can copy what they already have and just expand on it for my needs. LiveBinders is responsive and adaptable and, although has a slightly higher learning curve, the benefits of LiveBinders virtual file cabinet make bookmarking very clean and easy to navigate.

Using LiveBinders in an Academic Setting

Lesson/Activity: Collaborative Grant Writing

Common Core Standards: n/a

Details: The focus of this project is a practical application of one large project to include faculty, peers, and administrators. With funding at an all-time low, seeking funding through grants and donations is more important than ever before. This project is best developed in several small parts.

- Part 1: Create the initial binder with the first two tabs. Tab 1: Introduction to the purpose of grant writing. Tab 2: Tips and tricks for what makes a good grant. As a subtab, include websites that illustrate effective grant writing skills; encourage others to add tips and suggestions.

- Part 2: Add websites that provide links to valuable grant opportunities. Discuss who is applying for which grant so that everyone you are working with does not apply for the same grant. Record these in a separate tab using the text feature in LiveBinders, with a Google Doc, or offline.

- Part 3: Apply for grants. This step does not involve the binder.

- Part 4: Celebrate your success. On the next available tab, share your success stories or your learning opportunities. When the collection of stories is large enough, share these with your principal and even your superintendant as an example of the direct impact of the direct support librarians have on the learning community by providing new resources and opportunities to students.

- Part 5: Repeat as desired. Celebrate your accomplishments and then look for a new grant!

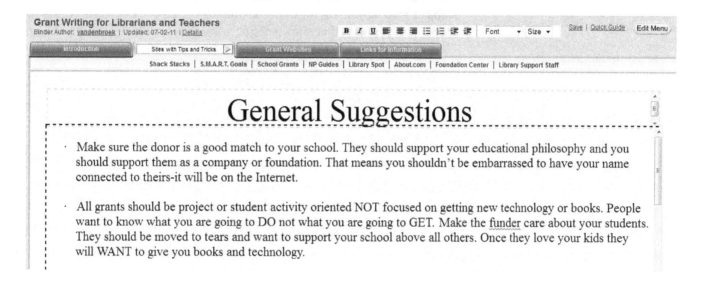

Required Preparation: Creating the binder.

Additional Technology Requirements: none

Tips and Suggestions: Start small. A group of 2 or 3 is a great start the first round. Think locally when applying for grants. Grants in your local area are typically more generous than are strangers, but may not provide as much money as a corporate sponsor.

Worksheets/Rubrics: n/a

Lesson/Activity: Author's Purpose

Common Core Standards: Craft and Structure 6.

Details: When I was in the classroom, my elementary students struggled with Author's Purpose. Part of the problem is that students don't intentionally look for this as they read. Exposing students to different text and teaching them what the different forms of purpose look like will help them to understand and recognize purpose when they read. Create a binder that has one tab each for the most commonly recognized purposes. Use the main tab area to display information about what makes that purpose different from the others, and then include links with clear examples as subtabs.

Required Preparation: Locate text that illustrates different types of purpose, create binder.

Additional Technology Requirements: none

Tips and Suggestions: A worksheet might help keep students focused if you are asking them to locate specific information from different sections, or this could just be an activity done as a group.

Worksheets/Rubrics: n/a

Lesson/Activity: Point of View

Common Core Standards: Craft and Structure 6.

Details: Point of view is initially difficult for students but then grows easier as they become more independent readers. Use point of view to help reinforce subject-verb agreement for upper-elementary students. Use LiveBinders to bookmark websites that show specific passages of subject-verb agreement. This can be from Internet articles or text created by the librarian. Have the students create a new tab and change the point of view in the story. For example, if the text is in first person, the students will change to third person or plural. Sometimes, verb tense will not change, sometimes it will. Discuss with students why this happens. For many students, switching tenses like this makes the verb tense in a textbook more concrete and approachable.

Required Preparation: LiveBinders, student accounts.

Additional Technology Requirements: n/a

Tips and Suggestions: Allow students having trouble with English grammar to work with partners or in small groups.

Worksheets/Rubrics: n/a

Lesson/Activity: That Was Then . . . This Is Now . . .

Common Core Standards: Key Ideas and Details 1 and 3.

Details: You've probably seen those birthday cards that point out how much has changed since you were born. Why not allow students to use the Internet to collect some of that data for themselves? Create a Live Binder with facts about the world when they were born versus the present world. Investigate:

- Population of that city and the world.
- Cost of houses.
- Cost of cars.
- Cost of food.
- Current events.
- Popular music/TV shows.
- Popular people.

Here are a few sites with useful information, but there are many other great websites available, especially if you have database access. Some databases will compare two years.

- U.S. Census: www.census.gov/
- On This Day (New York Times Archives): http://learning.blogs.ny times.com/on-this-day/

- InfoPlease: www.infoplease.com/yearbyyear.html
- Today in History Archives (LOC): http://lcweb2.loc.gov/ammem/today/archive.html

Required Preparation: Locate a few starter websites for students and help students create their own account.

Additional Technology Requirements: none

Tips and Suggestions: This will have the most impact with older students because more time will have passed since their birth, but if working with younger students, have them compare the current date to the year their teacher was born or when a parent or guardian was born.

Worksheets/Rubrics: n/a

Lesson/Activity: Art Styles

Common Core Standards: Integration of Knowledge and Ideas 7.

Details: Have students come to the library and research both in books and on the Internet, collecting information about one type of art style. Have them create LiveBinders that highlight both the style and those artists most known for using that style. Add video and pictures, where available. Students can work individually or collaboratively. Final projects can be shown in the library or in the classroom. Keep this resource from year to year and build a collection of student-generated research so that each year the collection of information expands.

Required Preparation: Pull books and help students set up LiveBinders accounts.

Additional Technology Requirements: Projector to show final projects.

Tips and Suggestions: Share the finished projects with history so that when a specific style is discussed, the history teacher will have examples to show students.

Worksheets/Rubrics: n/a

Lesson/Activity: Photography Basics and Website Tools

Common Core Standards: n/a

Details: The field of photography has come a long way and is now more digital than ever. Prepare a binder for use in art or for any school project requiring photography. Cover basic photography skills as well as how to modify photos with free photo imaging websites. Include:

- Camera settings.
- Getting the best shot.
- Lighting.
- Photo editing.
- File management (local or on hosting sites).

- Protecting ownership rights.
- Extra features on the camera like video.

Required Preparation: Locate and bookmark links.

Additional Technology Requirements: none

Tips and Suggestions: Display student creations in the library whenever possible.

Worksheets/Rubrics: n/a

Lesson/Activity: 4-H and Agriculture Links

Common Core Standards: n/a

Details: Show clubs like 4-H how to bookmark tools in LiveBinders. Students can create private binders that include websites with information on shows as well as informational websites. Using text, students can monitor the events they enter and record their progress like a virtual scrapbook. This can be turned in at the end of the season as proof of progress. 4-H sponsors can monitor student progress by joining their binders.

Required Preparation: Train students on LiveBinders and help them set up their own accounts.

Additional Technology Requirements: Scanner for awards and certificates.

Tips and Suggestions: LiveBinders will let you add supporting documents, so students can add scanned copies of awards and certificates to their binder.

Worksheets/Rubrics: n/a

Lesson/Activity: Instrument Introductions

Common Core Standards: n/a

Details: In our district, students choose instruments after a very brief introduction to them in fourth grade. Often, students are stuck with these instruments the entire rest of their academic career. Work with the orchestra and band teacher to create LiveBinders that showcase the different instruments. Find websites that discuss the pros and cons of each instrument. For fine arts schools focus on how students can build a career with that instrument. Use this LiveBinder during library time once students have checked out books or as a quick attention-getter.

Required Preparation: Locate and bookmark links.

Additional Technology Requirements: Projector is viewed whole group.

Tips and Suggestions: Be sure to incorporate video clips and sound clips of the instruments, even if it is just student samples.

Worksheets/Rubrics: n/a

Lesson/Activity: Sports Rules

Common Core Standards: n/a

Details: Part of the physical education curriculum requires students to learn the rules of basic games. Create a binder that covers the basic rules of the games and introduce these when you discuss nonfiction sports books. Compare the book, the information found on the websites, and the information provided by the athletics department. Allow students to locate videos on tutorial sites illustrating basic skills associated with a sport.

Required Preparation: Create a binder with basic sports rules and links to the sports section and sports biographies in your collection.

Additional Technology Requirements: none

Tips and Suggestions: Local umpires and other such officials know the rules inside and out. If possible, let students interview officials and post as supplemental material.

Worksheets/Rubrics: Worksheet 13: Sports Rules.

Lesson/Activity: Social Skills

Common Core Standards: n/a

Details: This is primarily geared towards younger students but could be adapted to any grade. As a class, discuss a book like *A Bad Case of Stripes* by David Shannon. Help the students predict the ending. Introduce the idea of being true to yourself, even when it is hard. Have students draw a picture of when they felt embarrassed. Talk about being brave. Show students the Live-Binder for other skills they might want to learn more about.

Required Preparation: Select a book for book discussion and create LiveBinder.

Additional Technology Requirements: none

Tips and Suggestions: This LiveBinder is introduced in the library but will be a huge help to teachers. If teachers don't accompany students to the library, make sure they understand the resource and know that they can add websites, as well.

Worksheets/Rubrics: Worksheet 14: Draw and Think.

Using Live Binders in a Public Library Setting

Service/Activity: Computer 101

Community Connection: Computer workshops for seniors or for novice computer users.

Overview: Seniors struggling with learning computer skills can complete a step-by-step introduction in the library, but frequently if they are using the skills at home will need an easy to navigate way to practice those skills. Develop an introduction to several different skills that beginning computer users could benefit from most. Consider topics such as creating and using a free e-mail account, using the different Microsoft Office programs or free programs like Google documents, how to navigate the library's online catalogue. If your library has systems in place for holds or interlibrary loans, be sure to include a tab for each of these.

Required Preparation: Either create a LiveBinders tutorial or choose one that has been already created.

Additional Technology Requirements: none

Tips and Suggestions: Consider using a website like Jing (www.techsmith. com/jing/) to enhance your LiveBinder. Jing creates a video that captures your keystrokes and screen movements as you complete the steps and allows you to talk at the same time. This is great for novice users because it provides both visual and audio examples. Jing will let you store this content locally or host on their site with a provided link that is easily embedded in a binder. See the tutorial in the appendix for more information or visit suggestion websites, such as Emergingedtech, for recommendations on similar video capturing sites (www.emergingedtech.com/2010/01/ comparing-12-free-screencasting-tools/).

Jing®   **Overview**   Free Version   Jing Pro    Download

 Take a picture or make a short video of what you see on your computer monitor.

 Share it instantly via web, email, IM, Twitter or your blog.

 Simple and free, Jing is the perfect way to enhance your fast-paced online conversations.

Worksheets/Rubrics: n/a

Service/Activity: Small Business Resources

Community Connection: n/a

Overview: Small businesses frequently need resources for their company. Many of these companies establish an informal mentorship with a more senior professional in their field, but patrons in small communities do not always have that luxury. Check with new entrepreneurs and brainstorm ideas of items they wish they had known before beginning their own business. Make a generic list of action/awareness items:

- Establishing a realistic budget.
- Creating business goals.
- Marketing.
- Branding and trademarks.
- Purchasing.
- Giving back to the community.

Required Preparation: Create a binder with the information detailed above.

Additional Technology Requirements: none

Tips and Suggestions: As an extension, look at the local statistics in your area and establish LiveBinders with resource tips for the top five new small business ideas. Focus on tips and tricks that are unique to that industry.

Worksheets/Rubrics: n/a

Service/Activity: Pet Care

Community Connection: Sponsor a pet adoption clinic.

Overview: Coordinate with the local animal shelter to have a pet adoption clinic outside of the library. Collect donations for rescue animal programs or service animals like Seeing Eye dogs. In the month prior to the event, have animal books on display as well as books on service animals. Create a LiveBinder with the help of the community, featuring information about different types of pets. Each pet should have two tabs. The first tab would be basic information on that animal, and the second would be information about how to care for that pet.

Required Preparation: Create a LiveBinder with links by pet, books for display.

Additional Technology Requirements: none

Tips and Suggestions: Stores like Petsmart allow pet adoption programs to come in quite frequently for free. Partner with this type of company to reduce costs and get free advertising for the event in their stores.

Worksheets/Rubrics: n/a

Service/Activity: Book Club Connections

Community Connection: Provides an information portal for book clubs that meet locally or virtually.

Overview: LiveBinders are a great place to keep the entire library's book club information in one place. One benefit for this is that individuals who normally only read one genre might venture to another one, since it only involves clicking on a different tab to see what is going on in other groups. Include websites of interest to these readers as well as any text about upcoming events. Allow patrons to post questions or comments.

Required Preparation: Create a binder with a different tab for each book club. Include information like meeting time, currently reading (don't forget to include an image), and other suggestions.

Additional Technology Requirements: none

Tips and Suggestions: You can set up a binder with access key if you want to protect younger users' content and set the browser as private.

Worksheets/Rubrics: n/a

Service/Activity: Patron-Created Book Reviews

Community Connection: Opportunity for patrons to waive a fine or, if budget allows, earn a free book.

Overview: Our local library allows students to get one free book a six-week period if they create a book review on a book not yet reviewed by another patron. An extension of this would be to allow patrons to post reviews on specific tabs. They would create an account in LiveBinders and have shared access to the binder. A benefit from this is that patrons can also add links to book websites and links to book trailers.

Required Preparation: Create a binder and allow patrons with LiveBinders accounts access to the created binder.

Additional Technology Requirements: none

Tips and Suggestions: The organization approach would depend on the size of the library. One binder might be enough for the entire library, or it might be better to do a different binder per genre so that the books can have their own tabs and subtabs of links, trailers, and movie connections related to that book.

Worksheets/Rubrics: n/a

Service/Activity: Car Enthusiasts

Community Connection: Coordinate with local car show.

Overview: Car shows happen almost every weekend, so why not invite participants to the library parking lot for a special after-hours event? Arrange for car enthusiasts to show off their cars and then invite them inside for refreshments and to show off the resources the library can offer. Have book displays about repairing cars as well as classic cars on display. Showcase any video collections that feature cars. Car enthusiasts spend a lot of time in their cars, so be sure to highlight your audio books. Focus both on fiction and nonfiction. On library computers, have LiveBinders ready to go with links that support their hobby. This can be a generic binder about cars or very customized to the audience attending.

Required Preparation: Create LiveBinder with introduction and basic content.

Additional Technology Requirements: none

Tips and Suggestions: Purchase small key chains, or get a dealership to donate, as a give away to anyone who signs up for a library card.

Worksheets/Rubrics: n/a

12

Web 2.0 Tech Tools Challenge: Diigo Tutorial

With the changes to Delicious, many users are transferring over to Diigo (pronounced Dee-go). While it is very easy once you are comfortable using Diigo, we've included this in the Tech Tools Challenge because it has greater potential and, as a result, a slightly higher learning curve. Diigo also extends social bookmarking to include personal learning networks. If you are unfamiliar with the phrase *personal learning network,* it is a collection of individuals or groups that you exchange information with in specific areas. You can participate in a personal learning network for any topic that interests you. What is so wonderful about this is that you do not have to be in nearby proximity. It is possible to have people in your personal learning network from any profession or from any part of the world.

Diigo also extends the use of Cloud-based technology by allowing you to download snips of a website or the entire page to review later. These images are stored in the Cloud. This allows the user to watch the evolution of a website, track community involvement on a wiki, and save annotation tools. This makes using the Internet possible even if the website is temporarily offline, making Diigo more of an eReader and less of just a bookmarking tool.

One con is that is does have ads in the free version. When working with younger students, you may have to watch for students inadvertently ending up in the wrong place. If you are an educator, remember to request an educator account after you sign up. If your school e-mail does not match their template, you will need to e-mail Diigo for help setting up this account. They are very quick to respond and the entire process takes only about a day.

Step 1: Create an Account

Click on **Join Diigo** and enter your account information as desired. This does require e-mail activation. You will want to use your school e-mail, but be sure to check your spam for the confirmation. Once you've signed up, click on the **Go Premium** icon at the top. Scroll down and click on the education basic plan. You will certainly want to apply for this, as it allows you unlimited bookmarks rather than limited. If it won't accept you school e-mail, Diigo is very responsive if you e-mail them.

Join Diigo

Step 2: My Library

Diigo calls their bookmarklet a *diigolet.* Kind of cute. If you are interested, you can drag this tool to your bookmarks bar or you can add the Diigo specific toolbar. On some computers, I could just use the diigolet, but on most I had to download the entire toolbar to have full functionality. This download may be blocked by your pop-up blocker or require administrator's rights. When you are finished, My Library is where your bookmarks and other tools are stored once you begin creating bookmarks.

My Library

This is the central place to store all your bookmarks, highlights, notes, pictures. For now, you haven't saved anything yet.

Option 1 - You can get started by adding diigolet to your browser

Diigolet is a "super bookmarklet" that allows you to highlight and add sticky-notes, in addition to simple bookmarking.

1. Make sure the "Bookmarks Toolbar" is visible. If it is not, go to menu View > Toolbars.
2. Drag this button: Diigolet up to your Bookmarks Toolbar.

Option 2 - Install feature-rich Diigo toolbar

Get feature-rich diigo toolbar »

Step 3: My Network

Initially your page will look like this:

If you are interested in establishing connections right away, you have a few options. You can search Diigo by name, e-mail, tag, site, URL, or using an advanced search.

Items from 0 People I follow

This is your network, which shows updates from people that you choose to follow. You can build friends lists to help you find good resources from people you trust and build your favorite network(s) accordingly.

To add people to follow:

- Search Diigo users of interest
- See if your friends are on Diigo
- Invite friends

Search Diigo users of interest

Don't let this stage overwhelm you. If you are nervous about trying something new, begin practicing with Diigo first, and then just join networks with individuals you know, such as teachers, patrons, or colleagues. Developing a personal learning network is important in a career, because we do not always have ample opportunities to work with other professionals. It is okay to start small and build out.

Step 4: My Groups

Groups are a quick way to set up collaborative work areas for coworkers or students.

What is Diigo Groups

Diigo Groups provides a ground-breaking collaborative research and learning tool that allows any group of people to pool their findings through group bookmarks, highlights, sticky notes, and forum.

 Create a group for your company, class, and teams.

 Interact in the group or on the web pages in-situ.

 Create a group knowledge repository.

Explore Diigo Groups

Find out what people are doing with Diigo Groups

[   ] [Search for a group]

Create a group - Step 1

| Step 1: Set up group | Step 2: Invite Others |

Group Name: [   ]
[Require minimum of 6 characters]

Group URL: http://groups.diigo.com/group/ [   ]
[Require minimum of 6 characters]

Description: [   ]
No more than 300 letters

Category:
- ⚪ Business & Finance
- ⚪ Computers & Internet
- ⚪ Cultures & Community
- ⚪ Entertainment & Arts
- ⚪ Family & Home
- ⚪ Games
- ⚪ Government & Politics
- ⚪ Health & Wellness
- ⚪ Collecting & Hobbies
- ⚪ Music
- ⚪ Recreation & Sports
- ⚪ Religion & Beliefs
- ⚪ Romance & Relationships
- ⚪ Schools & Education
- ⚪ Education - K12
- ⚪ Science
- ⚪ Travel
- ⚪ Video
- ⦿ Not Categorized

Who can view?
- ⦿ Public - anyone can view
- ⚪ Private - only group members can view

Searchable?
- ⦿ List this group in the search results
- ⚪ Do not list this group

How to join?
- ⚪ Open - anyone can join
- ⦿ Apply to join -- moderator approval required
- ⚪ By invitation only

Who can invite new members?
- ⚪ Only group moderator
- ⦿ All group members

[Create my group]   Cancel

First, name your group and set basic properties.

Next, invite others to join your group. You can skip this step if you want to until your work area is created.

Create a group - Step 2

✓ Your group has been created.

Step 1: Set up group | **Step 2: Invite Others**

Enter email addresses or your friends on Diigo:

Start typing a friend's name or email address.

You can also **choose from your Diigo address book** or **import from external address book**

Welcome Message:

Diigo will automatically include the group name, group description, and group URL in the email.

[Invite] [Skip]

Step 5: Community

This tab showcases the most bookmarks being booked most frequently by members of Diigo. These can range from random fun sites to educational sites.

Step 6: Bookmarking

After you set up your initial settings, you are ready to begin bookmarking. The Diigo bookmarklet takes up less space than the entire toolbar as it only shows up when you click on it, but it does have fewer options. Choose the one that best suits your needs. On the toolbar, you have many options.

Find the website you wish to bookmark. You can add the desired annotations before saving or save to annotate later. When ready, click **bookmark**. Fill in the details and the tags. Be sure to check the box if you want the bookmark to be private.

The bookmark will now show up on your Diigo account under the mylibrary page. Something to keep in mind when you are in Diigo and go to a website is that any changes you make will show up anytime you access that website, unless you log out of Diigo. That is incredible when you realize that all that data is stored in the Cloud. What that means is, if I work at home on Diigo bookmarks and then

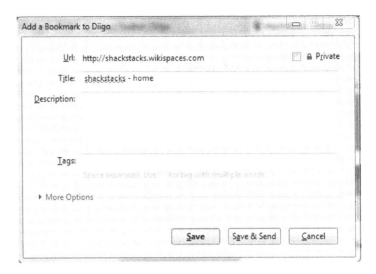

go to school, I will have the same annotations both places. Any changes I make at school will be there when I look at the website again at home. For that reason, it is important that students and patrons understand how to log in and out of the account successfully so that multiple users see only their own bookmarks, annotations, and comments.

Step 7: Annotation

There are quite a few tools when annotating in Diigo.

Bookmark: bookmark the page.

Highlighter: choose from one of four colors to highlight text. This is very helpful for long passages to focus the reader on a passage or link.

Capture: you can take a screen shot of a section or the entire text. Then you can also edit and point out specific details.

Send: allows you to forward over e-mail or other social networking sites.

Read Later: mark as an unread bookmark if you'd like to flag a link so you'll remember to go back to it. You can also then double click on the unread folder to view a bookmark that was marked read later.

Recent: any new bookmarks will show up in this folder.

Add a filter: set up filters for easy access to bookmarks by tag, list, recent, or unread.

Toolbar: this is set to default to the beginner settings shown below. The beginner settings give you most options but do not allow you to view comments or messages. Simply click those boxes to add.

Comments: this can be a whole-page comment or a floating-stick comment, as shown here.

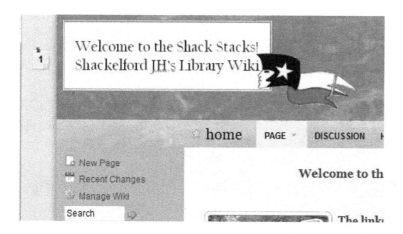

Messages: Shortcut to any messages within Diigo.

Step 8: My Lists

When in your Diigo account, you can create lists like you do in most bookmarking sites. Then you can specify which bookmarks go in which list. This might be something you want to set up at the onset if you aren't importing bookmarks in large numbers.

My Lists (0)

"List" is a great way to organize, share and display your specific collection of items.

+ Create new list

Step 9: Student Accounts

With the free educator account, you also have access to student accounts. In the library, if you set up generic student accounts, students can share this if necessary or individual teachers can create student accounts for their students. Read the help section on the website if you have trouble applying. It is very helpful and easy to follow.

Step 10: Diigo and Mobility

Diigo currently has apps for iPad, iPhone, Android, and Mac Quick Notes. On Apple devices, Diigo suggests using iChromy as the browser of choice. If you click on the tools link, you will have access to bookmarks, toolbars, app information, and more Web features.

13

Practical Application: Putting Diigo to Work

Diigo is in the Extending the Basics section because it includes all of the features we love from the other websites, as well as some powerful annotation tools. For an academic setting, the student accounts make using this website with classes much more realistic, because students do not need individual e-mail accounts. Diigo's tutorial (http://help.diigo.com) is very easy to navigate and is clear enough that even a beginning user can understand. The clear separation between personal and public links is also helpful.

One unique feature is that Diigo allows you to cache pages so that the entire content of the website is searchable rather, than just searching your tags. This is slightly limited in the free version, but there are enough pages allowed for you to know if that is a feature you will use regularly.

The personal learning network added in the most current version of Diigo is the winning feature by far. If used correctly, a personal learning network collects updates from a group of people you are interested in learning with collaboratively. While some librarians will be hesitant to try this form of electronic collaboration, it is less intimidating if you think of it like an electronic friendship. The more you grow together, the more you advance the field of librarianship and your own personal expertise.

Personal Use

I am not a Diigo expert, but am quickly falling in love. The first time I was introduced to Diigo, I thought it was pretty cool but wasn't sure how it would be practical. The more I use Diigo, the more impressed I am. The annotation features save me looking for data on websites I don't use frequently and make collaboration so easy. The added feature of a personal learning network keeps me learning every day.

When building my library wiki, I like to look at other librarians who have dynamic pages. While I look at sites, I can make notes about things I like and don't like on my page so I don't forget to change them when I go back. Diigo's capture option also allows you to take an image of the before and after of a website to track changes. If you are trying to prove increase usage of a wiki, this would be a great way to monitor changes.

Using in an Academic Setting

Lesson/Activity: Prior Knowledge before Novel Units Mini Research

Common Core Standards: Key Ideas and Details 1 and 2.

Details: Prior knowledge is incredibly important before starting a novel unit read together in class. This is especially important if the genre is new to students or is historical fiction that requires an understanding of the time period. Vocabulary is another important discussion point when building prior knowledge. If possible, divide this activity into three days.

Day 1: Research basic background information about the time period about which the book was written if historical fiction, or introduce some things that are unique to that genre. Bookmark valuable websites in Diigo and use the annotation tools to point out facts that students found most interesting. At the end of class, allow students to share the website they found the most helpful and two facts they learned. If the novel unit requires specific background information to cover vocabulary, make sure to focus the search. For example, if students were reading *Nory Ryan's Song* by Patricia Reilly Giff, students would need background information about potato famines, Ireland, the 1800s, and even broader topics like poverty. Refer back to these student-collected resources while reading the novel.

Day 2: Discover basic background information about the author. Consider things like other works they have written, childhood, interviews on the book, and so on. Show students how to locate the official author's website and bookmark on Diigo. Allow students to collect additional information about the author and use annotation tools to take notes about important facts. At the end of class allow students to share two things they learned that no one has mentioned yet.

Day 3: Look up facts definitions and example for tough vocabulary or new vocabulary. As the teacher, provide the list of online resources for vocabulary research. This can be on a generic Diigo account for the school. Students can use a Web organizer that helps students fully understand the meaning of the word. Enchanted Learning has a variety of templates on their website: www.enchantedlearning.com/graphicorganizers/vocab/.

Required Preparation: Adjust rubric as desired and collect resources for vocabulary definitions.

Additional Technology Requirements: none

Tips and Suggestions: If students are reading a classic, many of these now fall under creative commons and so the full text is available online through projects like Project Gutenberg (www.gutenberg.org) or as an eBook through sites like Free Classic Audiobooks (http://freeclassicaudiobooks.com/).

Worksheets/Rubrics: Rubric 4: Prior Knowledge Mini Research, for days 1 and 2.

Lesson/Activity: Color-Coding Parts of Speech

Common Core Standards: Language Progressive Skills 4b.

Details: Early elementary classes focus on directly teaching the parts of speech and then middle and junior high work on refining and applying this skill, but surprisingly I still have junior high students who don't know a pronoun from a noun. As a class, read short books that focus on a particular part of speech (verbs), and then go to Diigo and use the highlight feature locating and highlighting any word in that section that is a verb. Showcase a book on adjectives and then have students highlight the adjectives in a different color. There are four colors, so student can do up to four different parts of speech. Have students print the page in color and turn in to the teacher for a grade. Checkout the books used to the teacher for reteach as needed or for students to read during silent reading time.

Required Preparation: Bookmarks on Diigo that contain multiple examples of the parts of speech focused on during the lesson, student accounts in Diigo.

Additional Technology Requirements: n/a

Tips and Suggestions: You can also do this same activity with punctuation rules using books, websites, or online tutorial websites that illustrate punctuation in fun and creative ways. If you want to win over teachers, offer to grade the assignment for them. It's extra work for you but it really impresses teachers.

Worksheets/Rubrics: n/a

Lesson/Activity: Comparing Facts in Websites and Books

Common Core Standards: Integration of Knowledge and Ideas 7–9.

Details: This concept seems to stump our students the most. I think there are two main reasons for this. One, we don't do enough explicit teaching about how to read and compare information across multiple texts, unless it is a testing packet that we are having students complete. When students do poorly on a test packet, they simply learn that they aren't good enough at the skill. Unless the teacher remediates the skill, students don't have enough prior knowledge to know how to compare information across multiple texts. The second area I think causes trouble for students is that when they read a nonfiction text, they assume it is factual. That is part of the reason they have so much trouble determining validity. If you talk to a child about the difference between fiction and nonfiction, the message is clear: Fiction consists of pretend stories that are sometimes based on the truth but not enough to be considered fact; nonfiction, then, is the opposite because it is fact based. The extrapolation of that then is that everything in the nonfiction section is true, which we know is not a correct assumption due to bias, location of graphic novels, folk tales, and so on. When students look at the Internet, they see it as another authoritative nonfiction source, so it is critical that students understand how to determine fact from fiction.

For this activity use the combination of books and Internet resources to gather information across multiple texts. It is okay if your text has some bias because that is an important speaking-point for a mini lesson on author's purpose. Look at the books in your collection before you begin. Make sure you pull the most current ones, to avoid too much confusion. This activity may even remind you of the importance of weeding your collection for accuracy and bias.

As students research, have them use the comment feature in Diigo to mark difference between text and website as well as propose any questions or ideas they have when researching. When research concludes, have students share what they've learned by creating a mind map or concept map of the different ideas as a class using a free mapping website. Discuss their findings to make sure that students grasped not only the content but also the difference in the information presented in the different texts.

Required Preparation: Websites on Diigo and books on the same topic, preferably a new topic for every four students.

Additional Technology Requirements: Projector and an idea-mapping program such as Bubbl.us (https://bubbl.us/) or Mindmeister (www.mindmeister.com/).

Tips and Suggestions: It would work best to have at least two Internet resources for each book. If possible, have multiple websites and books so that when reviewing what students learn, the last students are able to contribute to the discussion.

Worksheets/Rubrics: n/a

Lesson/Activity: Favorite Author Contest

Common Core Standards: n/a

Details: Many students are chain-readers, meaning they read everything an author has written before moving on and consuming anything they can find by the next author. These could be books in a series or just other works written by that author. Capture this enthusiasm by hosting a contest where students create a Diigo that showcases their favorite author. Have a poll in the library or on the website where students nominate the winner.

Required Preparation: Diigo accounts.

Additional Technology Requirements: none

Tips and Suggestions: none

Worksheets/Rubrics: n/a

Lesson/Activity: Phonics Rules and Dictionaries

Common Core Standards: Phonics and Word Recognition 3.

Details: Phonics rules are very easy for some students to learn and seemingly impossible for others. Locate several website that practice phonics skills and bookmark them in Diigo. When students are close to mastering a skill, provide a random website that has lots of samples of that phonics rule in the writing style. Using the highlighter, students highlight the rules.

Required Preparation: Locate phonics practice websites and websites for proof of mastery.

Additional Technology Requirements: n/a

Tips and Suggestions: Make sure when looking for good phonics sites that the website uses conventional phonics and grammar rules. There are many English websites that use variant forms of spelling because they were created in Canada or England.

Worksheets/Rubrics: n/a

Lesson/Activity: Weight Loss Tips

Common Core Standards: n/a

Details: Although connected to the Health curriculum, most schools do not focus on weight loss, other than in athletics. Providing a list of resources for weight loss tips for students that can be viewed on their own time take some of the embarrassment out of classroom discussion. Create a list of websites that promote weight loss through healthy eating and regular exercise. Provide these links for students as a station in a Healthy Me unit that introduces students to books about nutrition and best practices. If school screenings leave excessive amounts of time waiting in line, this would be a great way for students to learn at the same time. If creating these links on a generic school account, ask the school nurse or local nursing student to add annotations for students that would be important tips or facts.

Required Preparation: Create bookmarks in Diigo.

Additional Technology Requirements: none

Tips and Suggestions: Work with the school cafeteria and plan this lesson during the time of the year when the cafeteria is most focused on healthy eating practices.

Worksheets/Rubrics: n/a

Lesson/Activity: Sight-Reading

Common Core Standards: n/a

Details: Learning how to read music is very important for any student wishing to excel in band, orchestra, or choir. When discussing your collection of books on famous musicians or nonfiction about instruments, introduce students to the Diigo bookmarks. Students can use their accounts to track their progress on learning to read music and as well as where they are struggling. Many websites contain full music pieces on the Internet. Students can mark the areas where they have trouble knowing what comes next, and work on recognizing those notes. The annotation tool is also a great way to add comments from the teacher.

Required Preparation: Create Diigo bookmarks.

Additional Technology Requirements: none

Tips and Suggestions: Include in the links interactive sites that allow students real-time feedback about their sight-reading abilities.

Worksheets/Rubrics: n/a

Lesson/Activity: Nursery Rhymes

Common Core Standards: Craft and Structure 4.

Details: While some students are familiar with nursery rhymes, many students no longer come to the first day of school with nursery rhymes in their reading histories. Create a list of nursery rhymes available online for early and emerging readers. As you introduce these books in the library, provide the user ID information to parents via a newsletter or weekly progress update, so that parents can become a part of the library's learning network and have access to the websites at home or at a local public library if parents do not have Internet access at home. If possible, have a special event where parents can come to the library and learn about Diigo.

As the readers mature during the year, use Diigo to evaluate and compare different versions of the same rhyme. When you look for differences, use books, Internet versions, or oral version students have learned from parents.

Required Preparation: Create Diigo links.

Additional Technology Requirements: Projector for whole group instruction, document camera for books.

Tips and Suggestions: Some nursery rhymes are available in SMART board format. If you have access to a SMART board consider this an alternative source of comparison.

Worksheets/Rubrics: n/a

Service/Activity: Writing Club and Fan Fiction

Community Connection: Support writing clubs.

Overview: If your library has a writing club, consider tapping into the power of fan fiction. Teenagers especially love creating fan fiction based on their favorite novel. Many fan fiction sites exist for showcasing patron work. Bookmark sites on Diigo that explain what fan fiction involves as well as sites about how to write fan fiction. In your writing clubs, have access to netbooks or laptops if possible so that members can evaluate fan fiction on a website using highlights or comments. Discuss what they enjoy most and what they enjoy least. Allow club members time for creation of their own fiction and, if desired, to post on a fan fiction website.

Required Preparation: Individual accounts.

Additional Technology Requirements: Laptops or net books.

Tips and Suggestions: Consider your audience when bookmarking fan fiction sites. Some fan fiction is a little racier than others and might not be appropriate for a younger audience.

Worksheets/Rubrics: n/a

Service/Activity: Books with Movie Connections

Community Connection: n/a

Overview: Create a display of books that have a movie based on the book. Use Diigo to bookmark information on the movie and then information on the book from your online catalog. Encourage patrons to create public comments that discuss the connection between the movie and the book as a comment.

Required Preparation: Collection of books, Diigo with book and movie links.

Additional Technology Requirements: none

Tips and Suggestions: Encourage patrons to recommend other books similar to the one they are reviewing for those who enjoyed the book.

Worksheets/Rubrics: n/a

Service/Activity: Recipe Changes

Community Connection: Ask a local restaurant to do a short cooking demonstration, discussing how to modify recipes.

Overview: We already focused on one activity about food, so here is a slight spin on that to show patrons. Arrange to have a local chef highlight a simple recipe they are willing to share with the public. Provide the link to the showcased recipe in Diigo and show patrons how to search for recipes online. Using Diigo's annotation tools, discuss ways to change the recipe to make it different or adjust for food allergies. Each individual can modify a recipe to include changes or make notes about vocabulary that is unfamiliar to them.

Patrons can also highlight tricky parts of a recipe, such as when the total amount of sugar is listed in the ingredient list but it is used in the recipe separately.

Using tags will help them keep similar recipes together. They can even include a link to a website like Linoit (http://en.linoit.com), where they can keep a shopping list as they look through websites. Linoit is a website that looks like a virtual corkboard. It allows you to add virtual sticky notes in a variety of colors so you can color code your grocery list or have multiple stores on the same page. This is a free website but does require e-mail. With Linoit, you can control the privacy settings to make it viewable by everyone, only a few, or no one but you.

Required Preparation: Have a Diigo account to show patrons and a handout for patrons, if desired.

Additional Technology Requirements: Projector.

Tips and Suggestions: n/a

Worksheets/Rubrics: n/a

Service/Activity: Cosmetology Careers

Community Connection: n/a

Overview: In your career section, provide a link to Diigo bookmarks showcasing popular careers in the field of cosmetology. Bookmark required prior experiences as well as local opportunities in that profession. Include tutorials or interviews with professionals in the trade. Showcase resources that patrons can check out on that subject area.

Required Preparation: Bookmarks on Diigo.

Additional Technology Requirements: none

Tips and Suggestions: Link to local regulations or requirements for state certification, where applicable.

Worksheets/Rubrics: n/a

Service/Activity: Website Creation

Community Connection: Website Creation Workshop.

Overview: Partner with a local computer expert to do a mini workshop on simple Web creation. Survey the patrons interested in the workshop to determine their skill set. This may require holding several different workshops to make sure that classes group individuals together with roughly the same amount of prior knowledge. Website building is something that can quickly overwhelm people. If too unequally matched, neither the advanced nor the inexperienced participant learn much in the session.

Using Diigo, create a basic list of website development bookmarks. Show patrons how to create their own list and how to use comments and highlights.

Required Preparation: Pull books and create initial Diigo bookmarks.

Additional Technology Requirements: Projector, access to computers for class.

Tips and Suggestions: By keeping their notes private, patrons can use the tutorial websites to make notes for later reference.

Worksheets/Rubrics: n/a

Service/Activity: Services for Low-Income Families

Community Connection: Food Drive or Coat Drive.

Overview: Collect a list of resources for struggling individuals and families by coordinating with local food pantries and housing authorities. Create a Diigo list of places and services than support low-income situations. Make sure to include the features offered by the library, like free Internet service and homework support for students, if applicable. Provide these resources on your website as well as through the services you are promoting.

Organize a local canned food drive or coat drive. When people donate or ask about resources, show them the list of resources in Diigo. Consider waiving small library fines for those individuals willing to donate.

Required Preparation: Bookmarks on Diigo grouped by tags for easy accessibility such as free_services, financial_assistance, food_banks, healthcare, and so on.

Additional Technology Requirements: none

Tips and Suggestions: Local churches, schools, laundromats, and apartment buildings are also good place to display information about the services at the library and in the community.

Worksheets/Rubrics: n/a

Service/Activity: Fitness Fun

Community Connection: Coordinate with the city as to be the start or end of a community run/walk event and provide refreshments.

Overview: Get involved with the next run/walk event hosted in your city. Ask volunteers to provide large umbrella tents and offer water and a place to cool off. Have bookmarks in Diigo available that focus on tips for runners or information about local trails and events. Make sure displays toward the front of the library contain both fiction and nonfiction books about running or walking so that it draws people into the library. Getting involved in an event like this helps the atypical library user understand that the library isn't always a whisper factory and that anyone is welcome.

Required Preparation: Purchase refreshments, create bookmarks on Diigo, arrange displays, and coordinate volunteers.

Additional Technology Requirements: none

Tips and Suggestions: Even though you have air conditioning, not everyone will come into the library. Have a flyer with library information or put a tag on the water bottle with library information and links.

Worksheets/Rubrics: n/a

Community Connection: n/a

Overview: Theater buffs will love the highlighting and comment feature of Diigo. If all members of a cast use the same login, they can view highlights of important sections of dialog. This could also be used to highlight changes to the script or blocking. The comment feature with floating sticky note could be used for a question-answer and the whole-page note used for adding the costuming and lighting information.

Required Preparation: Diigo account for showing Diigo to local production companies.

Additional Technology Requirements: n/a

Tips and Suggestions: n/a

Worksheets/Rubrics: n/a

14

Cutting-Edge Bookmarking: QR Codes

You might not be familiar with phrase *QR code*, but you've probably seen them and just not known what they were. This is a QR code. When you scan it with a QR code-reader, the code will take you to my library website.

Basically, a QR code is a two-dimensional barcode that can hold a limited amount of data. It typically points to a website, small amounts of text, such as address or phone number, or an e-mail address. A QR code will hold up to 7,089 total characters or 4,296 alphanumeric characters. That said, most of the online creators have you limit the text to approximately 250 characters to keep the code simple.

The great thing about QR codes is that you don't have to change the code unless the website changes. A Web address is static; the address doesn't change, but I can change the content on that website as often as I wish. For example, I can update my school website every day, but I don't need to generate a different QR code unless I change the address of my website.

To decode a QR code, you need a device with a camera to be able to read the QR code. Typically, this is a smartphone, iPad, or iPod Touch. Smart phones will have a downloadable app (tons of free ones) where you just scan the QR code and it shows you the data hidden in the code. You can also download QR code readers directly to your computer via a Web browser.

There are many free QR code creators on the Internet. There is no right or wrong option here. Simply find a website that creates a QR code that meets your needs. I use Kaywa, because it's very simple and does not require registration, so for the purpose of this tutorial, that is the creator we will use. Once you are comfortable with one, they all function pretty similarly.

Step 1: Create a QR Code

Go to the website http://qrcode.kaywa.com/.

Note that you have four options on the left-hand side. The first is for a website.

Simply enter the website URL you want to bookmark in the box. Then select your size (will depend on what you are doing with it). Select **Generate**. The QR code will appear in the box to the left. Here is what it looked like when I made the code shown earlier.

If you want to link to something other than a website, you have three other choices. You can select text, phone number, or SMS (think text message). The displays change with the different choices.

QR Code Generator for URL

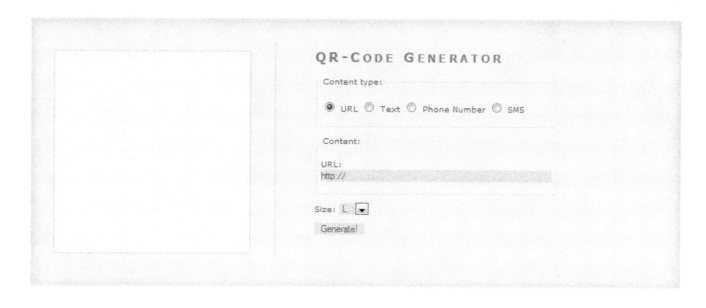

Sample of finished URL QR code

QR Code generator for text

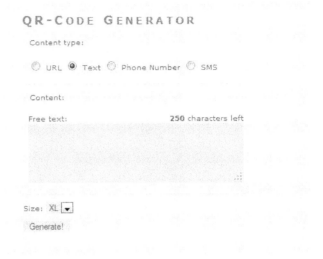

QR Code generator for a phone number

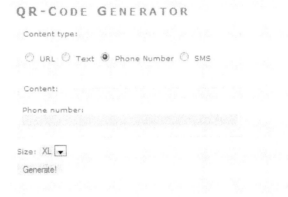

QR Code generator for SMS

Step 2: Use the Code

You can copy and paste the QR code into a document or you can save the QR code as a picture for later use. You can enlarge the QR code if you save it, but don't make it too large, because you have to be able to take a picture of it and if it is too large you won't be able to get it all on the screen. Remember that QR codes are static, so they do not change even if you change the content of the website. The only time you'd need to make a new QR code is if you change the address of a website.

Step 3: Consider Your Device

The cheapest device for library use is probably an iPod Touch, but if you have access to iPads, students will have an easier time reading the information on the screen. If your school allows, students can use their own smartphones, but that is a district decision. Our campus has QR codes posted around the school, with no notes other than "Scan me before or after school." Use of those websites has increased immensely, just due to student curiosity. For the sake of consistency, we will refer to the devices as iPods during this discussion.

Step 4: Download a QR Code Reader App

This choice is up to you, but consider consulting students and faculty for which one they are already comfortable using. The many free apps all work about the same. Some QR codes require specific readers, so if it doesn't work, you might try a different reader. Please don't pay for an app, though—you can find a great one at no cost!

Step 5: Teach, Teach, Teach

Use a handout or a demo lesson that focuses on the functions of a QR code. People are getting more used to seeing these around, but most people still view them as a little too geeky and are a little intimidated around them. You can quickly overcome this by posting QR codes in various locations and use them as teaching opportunities. The QR craze will catch on fast once people understand how easy they are to create and decode.

15

Practical Application:
Putting QR Codes to Work

Confession time. I recently purchased my very first eBooks for the library. The reason for the delay? I kept waiting for the eBook market to stabilize. I kept researching and trying to find out what the "best" option was and at the same time consulting others on how "best" to incorporate them into my library. What happened as a result was that the eBook market is just as confusing now as ever, but I missed a critical window of opportunity with some of my patrons by delaying. That was why I just jumped in. Even if it's not "right," it's an attempt, and sometimes with people it really is the effort rather than the result. How does this fit into a book about social networking? QR codes are the hottest new trend right now. They are very new but I expect to see more and more about them in the upcoming months and years. Large companies are now recognizing their validity and trying to take advantage of this technology, and so must we. Sure, it's a little gimmicky, but so what? If it gets the attention of people in a new way, it's worth the effort. These are just a few ideas to get you started.

Personal Use

Other than using QR codes to learn more about an object and just show off cool new technology, I haven't used QR codes that much for my personal bookmarks. I have thought about adding QR codes to my circulation counter to take me to websites I use the most, because they can be small and the scanner will still read them. Since a QR code takes you to any link the possibilities really are endless.

Using QR Codes in an Academic Setting

Lesson/Activity: Library Orientation

Common Core Standards: n/a

Details: Almost every librarian does a library orientation of some sort. Sometimes these are PowerPoint introductions, scavenger hunts, or simply a walking tour around the library. QR codes can give new life to these orientations by taking the fun of a scavenger hunt and proving information that can be accessible year round and not just during those first few weeks of school.

For this activity, you might consider laminating your QR codes for durability. You can leave them up for the entire year if you like and new students can complete the orientation as they arrive. You can mount them on cardstock if you'd like, for extra thickness. Check the QR code to make sure it scans before mounting. Sometimes a bubble in lamination or lighting in a specific area can affect scanability.

When students enter the library, pass out the worksheets. Allow students to work in small groups. This will help with the discomfort of being in a new location as well as require fewer code readers. Make one student in each group responsible for ensuring the iPods are handled properly. After students find their information, bring them back to discuss what they've learned and review by passing out QR code bookmarks.

Required Preparation: Create and display QR codes (and websites with information if needed).

Additional Technology Requirements: QR Code Reader on mobile device (like iPod touch, smartphone, or iPad).

Tips and Suggestions: In the Worksheet/Rubric section, you will find a sample QR code scavenger hunt for students, as well as sample Orientation Bookmarks. You can modify these for your own use or start from scratch. Although each librarian has unique expectations of what to cover in an orientation, Table 15.1 includes a few suggestions to get you started.

Worksheets/Rubrics: Worksheet 5: Library Orientation; Worksheet 9: QR Code Bookmarks.

TABLE 15.1 Orientation Suggestions

Area to Include in Orientation	*QR Suggestions*
Library Hours	QR code next to where your hours are displayed or on the library doors.
Librarian Information	QR code on your desk, on you as a name tag, or next to your Currently Reading List.
Catalog Information	QR code attached to the computer where you do circulation.
Available formats of books	Next to a display that you want to promote (ex., audio books), place a QR code highlighting all the ways you can read in the library.
Details on Circulation Rules	QR code by the scanners
Read-Alike Lists	Showcase popular books with QR codes suggesting other books students might enjoy.
Review of Library Policies	Bookmark provided to students at the end of the lesson, with a link to the library website where the rules are outlined. You can post your traditional PPT here if you think it would benefit students to see the information in another form. Also provide the website for parent convenience.

Lesson/Activity: Main Idea

Common Core Standards: Key Ideas and Details 2.

Details: Indentify short picture books that have a clear main idea with supporting details. For younger students, read the book and decide on the main idea in the class. Use a large easel with paper where students write down the topics discussed most in the book. For older students, allow them to generate their own ideas on a sticky note first before sharing with the group. They can write down ideas they hear a lot in the text and then decide what are supporting details and what are main details. Draw one name for each book and let the student scan the QR code that contains the answer to what is the main idea of the story.

Required Preparation: Pull books with clear main ideas and create text QR codes with answers.

Additional Technology Requirements: Easel with paper.

Tips and Suggestions: Easel is not the only way to tally results. A projector with graphing program would also be a great way of showcasing ideas.

Worksheets/Rubrics: Worksheet 11: Main Idea.

Lesson/Activity: Read and Listen Stations

Common Core Standards: Presentation of Knowledge and Ideas 5.

Details: This activity is perfect for both reluctant readers and early readers. If possible, spread out comfortable reading areas around the entire library so that students are less distracted. Place books by the reading areas with a scannable QR code located on a display of some kind. Inexpensive mini plastic photo frames are perfect for displaying QR codes, because you can slip new codes in and out very quickly. On the QR code, link to full text of the book or audio/visual retellings of the books.

Good websites for interactive reading:

- Storyline Online (www.storylineonline.net/) (free)—actors actually read the book.

- MeeGenius (www.meegenius.com) (free and paid)—Allows you to be read to or read on your own. Available as an app if your school has the appropriate devices.

- Tumble Books (http://tumblebooks.com) (subscription)—entire book with animations and voice-over text. Sometimes, the actual author reads the book.

- LibriVox (http://librivox.org/) (free)—audio books for older students from public domain.

Required Preparation: Locate books with an audio companion and create QR codes.

Additional Technology Requirements: Remember that if you are using an iPad, some of these eBook readers use Flash, so a browser like Cloud will help but isn't a perfect solution.

Tips and Suggestions: This type of activity would work well during a special after-school night to promote reading.

Worksheets/Rubrics: n/a

Lesson/Activity: Genre Read-Alike Lists

Common Core Standards: n/a

Details: As a librarian, you know the pressure of trying to help students blossom into the love of different genres. The desire to clone oneself is the strongest at these times because it is hard to discuss every book with all the patrons you serve. This is where Read-Alike Lists or displays can come in handy. Follow what books students read in class as well as watching the library circulation for popular books and themes.

You can use QR codes to link to a website where others have already created fabulous lists. If you Google read-alike lists and the book, you will be amazed at the quality of lists already present. A downside to using someone else's list is that you may not have all the books on their list. You can create your own list using a site like Glogster (http://edu.glogster.com) or Wix (http://wix.com). A third option is to link to sites that recommend other books. Students type in a book they enjoyed and then the site will make recommendations. Spelling is important on these, so it helps if students have the books in front of them. Book Seer is the most popular of these sites.

Samples of Lists Created by Others

http://americanlibrariesmagazine.org/news/ala/yalsa-offers-readalikes-mockingjay

http://readingtub.pbworks.com/w/page/13341506/Read-Alikes-by-Audience

Samples of Librarian-Created Lists

www.wix.com/Vandenbroek/Readalikelist

Websites that Recommend Other Books

http://bookseer.com/

www.librarything.com/suggest

www.whatshouldireadnext.com/

Required Preparation: Locate or create read alike lists and QR codes.

Additional Technology Requirements: QR Code Reader on mobile devices (like iPod Touch, smartphone, or iPad).

Tips and Suggestions: none

Worksheets/Rubrics: n/a

Lesson/Activity: About the Author

Common Core Standards: n/a

Details: Publishers are beginning to include QR codes on book jackets, but a quick way to help students locate information on authors would be using QR codes. The link to the book website or author website can be printed and taped into the back of the book. As the author updates the website and writes additional books, the information would be easily accessible to students. This would be particularly helpful when trying to keep track of books in a series.

Required Preparation: QR codes and content.

Additional Technology Requirements: QR Code Reader on mobile devices (like iPod Touch, smartphone, or iPad).

Tips and Suggestions: As a fun attention-getter, you can have a picture of a popular author (especially fun if they have baby pictures posted on their websites) and then the QR code could link to their books and biography.

Worksheets/Rubrics: n/a

Lesson/Activity: Students Check Answers

Common Core Standards: Varies depending on subject.

Details: Group work and discussion in the library can get an extra boost by using QR codes. Instead of grading the activities when doing group work, available QR codes at the end of each section allow students to check their work. For example, when completing the Jog the Web exercise on Internet Validity you could add images that had the QR code. This prevents students from peeking at the answers before desired.

Required Preparation: QR codes.

Additional Technology Requirements: QR Code Reader on mobile devices (like iPod Touch, smartphone, or iPad).

Tips and Suggestions: When working in groups, monitor so that one student does not get to scan all of the answers. From past experience, I've learned that students tolerate physical differences between peers more readily than technological deficiency. When one student struggles with technology, a more-proficient student will take over the technology. Consider children who get frustrated at the speed of a parent texts and grab the phone to finish it for them.

Worksheets/Rubrics: n/a

Lesson/Activity: Vocabulary Word of the Day

Common Core Standards: Craft and Structure 4.

Details: Help teachers to create a display in the library with a fixed QR code that links to a website where you post a vocabulary word of the day. This can also be posted on your library website and can easily be mailed to administrators and board members as a fun way to promote collaboration in the library.

Required Preparation: QR code and content.

Additional Technology Requirements: QR Code Reader on mobile devices (like iPod Touch, smartphone, or iPad).

Tips and Suggestions: If you have student helpers, they can create a vodcast or podcast discussing the word and giving examples.

Worksheets/Rubrics: n/a

Lesson/Activity: Speed Booking

Common Core Standards: Comprehension and Collaboration 1.

Details: An exciting way to promote reading with older students is Speed Booking. Think speed dating, except instead of another person, students are getting to know a book, genre, or author. When students enter have 6–8 tables set up with one book on each table. Students will rotate from table to table, getting to know the book on each table and completing the handout (see handout section). Students can scan a QR code directing them to different elements that might entice them:

- Author information.
- Book reviews.
- Librarian created read alike list that features the book with other books they might know.
- Summary.
- Book website.
- Book trailer (can be librarian created or consider one of the sites listed in the Resource List).

- Podcast.
- Website that contains information on that topic.

Required Preparation: Handout, pull books, QR codes and content.

Additional Technology Requirements: QR Code Reader on mobile devices (like iPod Touch, smartphone, or iPad).

Tips and Suggestions: Although it is more complicated, when doing an activity like this, it works best if you have different books for each period. That way, at the end of class, those books can actually be checked out. This takes preparation, but it is well worth it. This is a perfect opportunity to focus on any genre you see not circulating well. It works well to have fiction, nonfiction, and poetry.

Worksheets/Rubrics: Worksheet 6: Speed Booking.

Lesson/Activity: Tutor Information

Common Core Standards: n/a

Details: Most schools bring in tutors who help with struggling students at some point during the academic school year. Typically, these tutors focus on students needing help passing standardized test scores, but sometimes they tutor in music, or even as a part of a general program of support for all students.

It is important to keep these tutors current on school information, as most do not have school e-mail. One way to do this is through the use of QR codes that link to a website for tutors. Create the code at the beginning of the year on a business card, with all the contact information for their sponsor. During the year, the tutors need only scan the QR code to be redirected to a site with updated information about that week.

Required Preparation: QR code linking to a basic page of tutor information, business card with QR code, and contact information.

Additional Technology Requirements: none

Tips and Suggestions: Those tutors who do not have a QR code reader or camera on their computer can go directly to the website for information.

Worksheets/Rubrics: Worksheet 12: Tutor Business Cards.

Lesson/Activity: Parent Resources

Common Core Standards: n/a

Details: Outside of our counselor's office sits a brochure rack with parent resources on a variety of different topics. These are intended for parents but are also used by students. Work with the counselors and add QR code links to resources you have in the library to support these topics. These can be taped directly to the box with the brochure. If your districts policy won't allow parent checkout, consider setting aside a time where parents can come read these resources before or after school in the library. This might also be a great time to reconsider policies that limit collection and computer usage with administrators.

Required Preparation: Create QR codes that link to library catalog.

Additional Technology Requirements: none

Tips and Suggestions: Parents may not be familiar with your library policies. Have a brochure ready that can be taken home for future reference.

Worksheets/Rubrics: n/a

Lesson/Activity: Weekly Professional Development for Teachers

Common Core Standards: n/a

Details: The relationship between teacher and evaluator is only as strong as the positive communication. Help administrators create a basic page that they can update once a week. This website should include general teaching tips, classroom management suggestions, highlight a different success story each week, and give examples of what principals hope to see on classroom walkthroughs.

Required Preparation: Creation of the website and the QR code.

Additional Technology Requirements: Cameras for teachers who do not have QR code readers of some sort.

Tips and Suggestions: Consider making the QR code into mouse pads for teachers. This can be done relatively inexpensively and is a very visual reminder about self-improvement. Check with the vendor before mass production to make sure they scan correctly.

Worksheets/Rubrics: n/a

Using QR Codes in a Public Library Setting

Note: The Additional Technology requirements include a QR code reader; however, in a public library setting that may not be required if patrons are required to supply their own QR code reader.

Service/Activity: Staff Book Recommendations

Community Connection: n/a

Overview: Sometimes, patrons are reticent to ask for recommendations but most public libraries have book displays. One way to use QR codes in the library would be to have a book display with the name of the librarian and the recommended book, with a QR code that links to other recommended books or even activities that librarian sponsors (i.e., book clubs, video clubs, etc.).

Required Preparation: QR code and content.

Additional Technology Requirements: QR Code Reader on mobile devices (like iPod Touch, smartphone, or iPad).

Tips and Suggestions: Instead of using the QR code creator we've been using, consider a site like QR Hacker (www.qrhacker.com/), which will allow you to add an image in the middle of the code or as a background. This will make the QR code a little more visible to patrons.

Worksheets/Rubrics: n/a

Service/Activity: Library Club Information

Community Connection: Outreach for library clubs.

Overview: When creating flyers for events, add a QR code to the bottom of the flyer as a link to the library website where you provide more detailed information. Another option is to display books on the topic and then use a QR code to give information on the club that goes with those books. For example, a Manga display could provide information about an upcoming club event.

Required Preparation: QR codes and content.

Additional Technology Requirements: QR Code Reader on mobile devices (like iPod Touch, smartphone, or iPad).

Tips and Suggestions: Mount QR codes on colored cardstock that includes your library logo. This will make them more uniform and help them appear a part of your library promotions rather than just a casual display. Put QR code explanation flyers on library doors, so patrons will know what all those QR symbols mean.

Worksheets/Rubrics: Worksheet 10: QR Code Overview.

Service/Activity: Volunteer Opportunities

Community Connection: Community involvement.

Overview: Many times community members want to be involved and are willing to volunteer but don't know where to start. Create a Glogster page (www.glogster.com) with links to ways individuals can volunteer. Glogster is a free website that allows you to create virtual posters. Don't forget to include ways to help your library. Try to focus on ways to volunteer that involve very little expense to the volunteer. In these tough economic times, more individuals are able to give time than financial resources. Display the QR code on your community board or next to a display of biographies on contemporary or historical philanthropic figures.

Required Preparation: Create a Glogster page and QR code.

Additional Technology Requirements: none

Tips and Suggestions: Find as many resources as possible for the initial Glogster page. You can add or remove volunteer opportunities based on patron feedback. If patrons tell you their experiences are all negative, that might not be a location you want to recommend.

Worksheets/Rubrics: n/a

Service/Activity: Career Development

Community Connection: n/a

Overview: In some libraries, the reference career section is actively used, and in others it is just a dust magnet. Use QR codes as a way of promoting this collection. Have different career books on display near QR codes that provide links to websites with more information. These can be websites you create or links to ones on the Internet. If you find a lot of valuable websites, use the QR code to link to a Sqworl page containing those links so it can be accessed on mobile devices.

Required Preparation: Locate links and create display.

Additional Technology Requirements: none

Tips and Suggestions: If skill level varies significantly, have two QR codes. One that has the information about the job and helps people choose that career, and one that provides links to websites that discuss career development or training in those specific areas.

Worksheets/Rubrics: n/a

Service/Activity: Community Events

Community Connection: Local contact with chamber of commerce or tourist information bureau.

Overview: Talk to your Chamber of Commerce or even visit nearby rest stops and pick up brochures for popular activities in your town. Use that information to develop a display. Suggest popular community events, books they might like if they enjoy those events, and then create QR codes for local websites. This is a great opportunity for patrons to get involved. Offer to waive a fine or give a longer checkout time if they create their own activity/book/QR code list.

Required Preparation: QR codes and content.

Additional Technology Requirements: QR Code Reader on mobile devices (like iPod Touch, smartphone, or iPad).

Tips and Suggestions: Mount flyers and QR codes on foam board of various thicknesses so they will extend off the wall and have a three-dimensional effect.

Worksheets/Rubrics: n/a

Service/Activity: Partner Reading Activities

Community Connection: Community Reading Promotion.

Overview: Promotion of One Book reading programs.

Required Preparation: If your library does a community read each year where all residents read the same book, the QR code is a great way to update stats and provide information. QR code ads can be placed in the paper or on local flyers without much information provided. The mystery of the QR code might entice those who wouldn't be excited about reading a book initially and hook them in by providing information about the book and how many people have already read the book.

Additional Technology Requirements: QR Code Reader on mobile devices (like iPod Touch, smartphone, or iPad).

Tips and Suggestions: Consider linking to LiveBinders, with a different tab containing information on the current year and previous books. If desired, include a page where patrons can nominate books for the next year.

Worksheets/Rubrics: n/a

Service/Activity: Heritage Months

Community Connection: Celebration of different heritages.

Overview: When celebrating events like Black History month or Cinco de Mayo, a photographic display of prominent figures with QR codes will engage patrons. One QR code can like to biographical information on the author and one can like to books you have in your collection about that individual or by that individual. You can feature popular pictures that people will find easily recognizable or more obscure pictures like an outline/shadow or even lesser-known childhood pictures. If possible, include a broad range of people like government, political, athletes, musicians, writers, and so on. Displays should include both historical and contemporary individuals. Younger patrons especially need to realize that these heritage months are for the living as well as *in memoriam.*

Required Preparation: QR codes and content, images, pull display books.

Additional Technology Requirements: QR Code Reader on mobile devices (like iPod Touch, smartphone, or iPad).

Tips and Suggestions: Contact city council or legislature members who would like to participate in these Heritage Months and include them in the displays.

Worksheets/Rubrics: n/a

16

Conclusion

Now that you've learned a little bit about different social bookmarking tools, you can see that they have their similarities and differences. Remember to not get overwhelmed. Look at the current needs of your library or your patrons and determine one or two sites that have the most direct impact on your personal and professional bookmarking needs. Here is a quick review of the different bookmarking features of each site.

- **Delicious**—storing all your bookmarking from multiple computers, creating stacks, networking, and sharing. Allows you to tag your links and compare to others who used the same tags. Also provides links in embeddable form.

- **LaterThis**—bookmarking websites you'd like to evaluate in more detail. Can add tags, comments, and rate.

- **Sqworl**—create groups of bookmarks on topics. It provides a picture representation of the link rather than text. Can collaborate by viewing other individuals who have similar links or search links by subject.

- **Jog the Web**—group text and links by topic. Can only be maintained by one person but has easily added text and personalization. Sequential layout is easy to follow. Website uses frames but has link to main website if needed. Can search through jogs created by others. Has a more international audience, so has links and tutorials in multiple languages.

- **LiveBinders**—virtual binders of bookmarks for public or private use. Can be shared and edited with anyone who has a LiveBinders account. Contains a dynamic database of user-created links, some of which allow you to copy and revise binder content.

- **Diigo**—bookmarking for lists or entire collection. Contains annotation and highlighting as well as a personal learning network. Allows storing of several offline pages for later review.

- **QR Codes**—2-D barcodes you create that link to more information. Requires a device with a camera and a QR code reader to use.

Step 1: Learn the Website

Take time to get very comfortable with the website. Create projects just for practice and revise and adjust as needed. The more comfortable you are with the website, the easier it is to use.

Step 2: Share the Website

Research proves that only part of our learning is by doing, part is by teaching. Find a collaborative partnership and share what you've learned. Undoubtedly, they will ask questions you didn't think about and together you can master the website. If in an academic setting, choose as your partner the person with whom you plan to co-teach . If they are invested in the learning, they will also be invested in the outcome.

Step 3: Use the Website with Patrons

You're a pro now, so jump on in there with your audience. They may know more than you on some points but that is okay. Allow yourself the privilege of learning from each other. It's okay to start small, just as long as you start! You can do it!

Worksheets and Rubrics

WORKSHEET 1 (Lesson Plan Template)

Dates:	Content Area:	Grade Level:

Lesson Title:

Common Core Objectives:	Prior Knowledge:

Lesson Overview with Description of Final Project:

Materials:	Resources, Handouts, or Websites:

Activity Description:

Lesson Reflection:

TAXES CAN BE TOUGH!

Check out this great link:

‹website here›

Need extra help? See if you qualify:

http://www.irs.gov

TAXES CAN BE TOUGH!

Check out this great link:

‹website here›

Need extra help? See if you qualify:

http://www.irs.gov

TAXES CAN BE TOUGH!

Check out this great link:

‹website here›

Need extra help? See if you qualify:

http://www.irs.gov

TAXES CAN BE TOUGH!

Check out this great link:

‹website here›

Need extra help? See if you qualify:

http://www.irs.gov

TAXES CAN BE TOUGH!

Check out this great link:

‹website here›

Need extra help? See if you qualify:

http://www.irs.gov

TAXES CAN BE TOUGH!

Check out this great link:

‹website here›

Need extra help? See if you qualify:

http://www.irs.gov

TAXES CAN BE TOUGH!

Check out this great link:

‹website here›

Need extra help? See if you qualify:

http://www.irs.gov

TAXES CAN BE TOUGH!

Check out this great link:

‹website here›

Need extra help? See if you qualify:

http://www.irs.gov

Student Name: _____ *Date:* _____

The two links I found the most helpful:

1. _____

2. _____

The two links I found confusing or unhelpful:

1. _____

2. _____

Two new links I would like to suggest adding for next year:

1. _____

2. _____

Other thoughts or suggestions:

_____

Student Name: _____ *Date:* _____

The two links I found the most helpful:

1. _____

2. _____

The two links I found confusing or unhelpful:

1. _____

2. _____

Two new links I would like to suggest adding for next year:

1. _____

2. _____

Other thoughts or suggestions:

_____

Please complete as much of the following information and then turn in this form to a librarian or drop it in the suggestion box.

Event Name: _____

Date: _____

Audience: _____

Cost: _____

Website: _____

Other important information: _____

Your name (in case of questions) _____

Phone or e-mail: _____

Please complete as much of the following information and then turn in this form to a librarian or drop it in the suggestion box.

Event Name: _____

Date: _____

Audience: _____

Cost: _____

Website: _____

Other important information: _____

Your name (in case of questions) _____

Phone or e-mail: _____

LIBRARY ORIENTATION: THE QR WAY!

You may answer these questions in any order. Return to your seat when you have answered all the questions and complete the bottom section by yourself.

1. How many weeks can you check out books? _____

2. How many books can you check out at one time? _____

3. What is the name of your librarian? _____

4. What types of reading can you do in the library? _____

   _____

5. What is the web address of the online catalog? _____

6. What is the web address of library's eBooks? _____

7. Is the online catalog the same as the library website? _____

8. What are your username and password for the online catalog and eBooks? _____

9. What happens if you turn in books late? _____

10. Where can you read for fun? _____

11. What are the titles of three magazines in the display?

    a. _____

    b. _____

    c. _____

12. What is the Texas Lone Star List? _____

Personal Questions (complete at table on your own):

1. What is your favorite kind of book to read? (You must pick something that interests you) _____

2. About how many books did you read last year? _____

3. What is one thing I should know about you as a reader? _____

 From *Bookmarking: Beyond the Basics* by Alicia Vandenbroek. Santa Barbara, CA: Linworth. Copyright © 2012

Name: _____

Teacher _____

Period: _____

SPEED BOOKING LOG

Directions: "Meet" your book and discuss:

- Use the book: cover, summary, reviews, labels, and so on.

- Use friends: has anyone read this book, other books by this author, or a book in this genre?

- Use your resources: What is provided to help you decide?

- Write a short summary of the book (what is it about) and what interests you or doesn't interest you about the book. "I liked it" is not enough information.

- Rate it between 1 and 5 stars. You may give it a partial star, but every book must have at least a partial star. (5 is the highest rating, the best it can be rated.)

- Your opinions do not have to match those of your group, but they can.

- When the timer goes off, we will be rotating in a clockwise direction as we give our reviews.

Note: Only write in the Table #1 blank if you are sitting at Table 1. ☺ Your table number is in the middle of your table

Table Number	One or two sentence summary of the book (what is it about) and one sentence about what you like or don't like.	Rate it! 1 to 5 stars (your opinion)
Table #1		☆☆☆☆☆
Table #2		☆☆☆☆☆
Table #3		☆☆☆☆☆
Table #4		☆☆☆☆☆
Table #5		☆☆☆☆☆
Table #6		☆☆☆☆☆
Table #7		☆☆☆☆☆
Table #8		☆☆☆☆☆

PERMISSION SLIP TO POST ACTIVITIES AND PROJECTS

Exciting things are going on in the library! Please find the permission slip below to post student work on the library website in celebration of all their academic success. These activities and projects are used throughout the year to promote literacy and reading appreciation.

Please e-mail me if you have any questions (insert e-mail).

Name of Student: _____

Please Choose One:

• One-time permission only.

    ☐ Description of Work _____

• Yearlong permission given for any student projects.

• Other: please specify _____

_____   _____

Student Signature   Date

_____   _____

Parent Signature   Date

WORKSHEET 8   Password Tracker

Website	User ID	Password	E-mail	Use

WORKSHEET 9: QR CODE BOOKMARKS

Shack Library
Library Links!

Online Catalog:

User ID:———————

Password:———————

Librarian: Miss Vandenbroek (Miss V).

http://desiny.aisd.net

Ebooks:

User ID above

https://wbb01131.follettshelf.com

Online Databases:

(see Miss V)

http://aisd.net/webresources

Shack Library
Library Links!

Online Catalog:

User ID:———————

Password:———————

Librarian: Miss Vandenbroek (Miss V).

http://desiny.aisd.net

Ebooks:

User ID above

https://wbb01131.follettshelf.com

Online Databases:

(see Miss V)

http://aisd.net/webresources

Shack Library
Library Links!

Online Catalog:

User ID:———————

Password:———————

Librarian: Miss Vandenbroek (Miss V).

http://desiny.aisd.net

Ebooks:

User ID above

https://wbb01131.follettshelf.com

Online Databases:

(see Miss V)

http://aisd.net/webresources

Seen me?

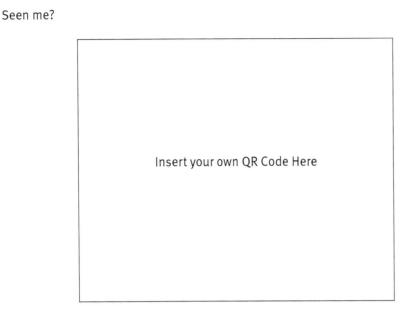

Insert your own QR Code Here

I'm a QR Code—a fancy name for a 2D barcode.

I can contain links to important information like:

- Phone numbers

- Addresses

- Text (more information on whatever I'm near)

- A website link

To decode my message:

- Download a free QR code reader app on your smart phone, iPod Touch, or iPad.

- Scan the code (make sure to open the app first)

See a QR Code Expert (aka: a librarian) if you need help!

Book 1

Title: _____

Words or Ideas Used Frequently:

Main Idea:

Supporting Details:

Book 2

Title: _____

Words or Ideas Used Frequently:

Main Idea:

Supporting Details:

Insert your own QR code here	Sponsor Name School Name School Address City, State, Zip Phone Fax Contact E-mail Website for tutors
Insert your own QR code here	Sponsor Name School Name School Address City, State, Zip Phone Fax Contact E-mail Website for tutors

Insert your own QR code here	Sponsor Name School Name School Address City, State, Zip Phone Fax Contact E-mail Website for tutors
Insert your own QR code here	Sponsor Name School Name School Address City, State, Zip Phone Fax Contact E-mail Website for tutors

Insert your own QR code here	Sponsor Name School Name School Address City, State, Zip Phone Fax Contact E-mail Website for tutors
Insert your own QR code here	Sponsor Name School Name School Address City, State, Zip Phone Fax Contact E-mail Website for tutors

Insert your own QR code here	Sponsor Name School Name School Address City, State, Zip Phone Fax Contact E-mail Website for tutors
Insert your own QR code here	Sponsor Name School Name School Address City, State, Zip Phone Fax Contact E-mail Website for tutors

Insert your own QR code here	Sponsor Name School Name School Address City, State, Zip Phone Fax Contact E-mail Website for tutors
Insert your own QR code here	Sponsor Name School Name School Address City, State, Zip Phone Fax Contact E-mail Website for tutors

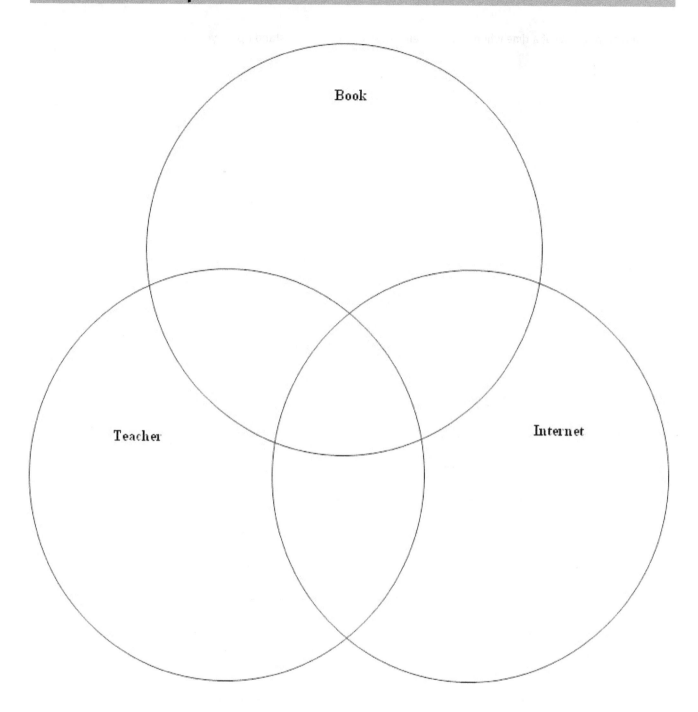

Book

Teacher

Internet

WORKSHEET 14 Draw and Think

Draw a picture below of a time when you were embarrassed or couldn't stand up for yourself:

What did you do to solve the problem?

Website URL: _____

Creator: _____

	4	3	2	1	0
Access	Viewable at the school (not blocked by the school filter).	Can view the interactive parts of the website at school.	Can view part of the website at school.	Can view very little of the website at school.	Unable to view at school (blocked by filter).
Downloads	Can access on school computers without any new downloads.	Can access with only minimal updates.	Can access part of the website without updates.	Requires excessive updates or downloads.	Requires a site license.
Passwords/e-mail	No log in required.	Log in required but no e-mail.	Log in required but no confirmation via e-mail.	Requires e-mail confirmation.	Subscription based service.
Content	Content is accurate and extends what we are learning in class.	Content is accurate and matches what we are covering in class.	Content is general and includes some of what we are learning in class.	Content is confusing or not well written.	Content seems to have errors or contradict what we are learning in class.
Interactive	Entire website is engaging and interactive.	Most of the activities are engaging and interactive.	Half of the website is engaging and interactive.	Little of the website is engaging or interactive.	The website is not interactive or engaging.
Authoritative	The website is authored by an authority in that area.	The website is a collection of other websites that are authoritative.	The website seems to have good content, but I can't tell who created the site.	The website was not created by an authoritative source.	Hoax (or made up) website.

Part 1: SQWORL!

	4	3	2	1	0
Teacher Approval	Topic covers approved science concept.	Student covers 95%–81% of assigned topic.	Student covers 80%–71% of approved topic.	Student covers 70% or less of approved topic.	Student researches an unapproved topic.
Content	Contains 10–15 websites on the chosen topic.	Contains 8–9 websites on the chosen topic.	Contains 7 websites on the chosen topic.	Contains 6 websites on the chosen topic.	Contains 5 or less websites on the chosen topic.
Interactive	Contains 4 interactive websites.	Contains 3 interactive websites.	Contains 2 interactive websites.	Contains only 1 interactive website.	Contains 0 interactive websites.
Video	Contains 2 video clips.				Contains 1 or less video clips.
Definition	Includes a definition of the concept.				Does not include a definition of the concept.

Part 2: Questions

	4	3	2	1	0
Questions	Includes 10 questions with 5 or more showing higher level questioning strategies.	Includes 9 questions with 5 or more showing higher level questioning strategies.	Includes 8 questions with 4 or less showing higher level questioning strategies.	Includes 7 questions with 3 or less showing higher level questioning strategies.	Includes 6 or less questions or no higher level questioning strategies.
Spelling	Questions contain no spelling or grammar mistakes.	Questions contain very little spelling or grammar mistakes.	Questions contain a few spelling or grammar mistakes.	Questions contain multiple spelling or grammar mistakes.	Questions contain excessive spelling or grammar mistakes.

Part 3: Answer and Evaluate

	4	3	2	1	0
Completes questions	Answers all of the proposed questions or provides clear explanation as to why that answer is not available.	Answers 80% of the proposed questions or provides clear explanation as to why that answer is not available.	Answers 70% of the proposed questions or provides clear explanation as to why that answer is not available.	Answers 60% of the proposed questions or provides clear explanation as to why that answer is not available.	Answers 50% of the proposed questions or provides clear explanation as to why that answer is not available.
Feedback	Feedback is positive and beneficial to the learning process.	Feedback is positive and adds somewhat to their partner's learning.	Feedback is positive but adds little to their partner's learning.	Feedback is negative.	No feedback is given.

Student Name: _____

Discovery: _____

	4	3	2	1	0
Mathematical Content	Content is accurate covers four important facts.	Content is accurate and covers three important facts.	Content is accurate and covers two important facts.	Content is accurate and covers one important fact.	Content not accurate or has no facts.
Background Content	Content is accurate covers four important facts.	Content is accurate and covers three important facts.	Content is accurate and covers two important facts.	Content is accurate and covers one important fact.	Content not accurate or has no facts.
Impact to Mathematics	Content is accurate, covers three or more important contributions.	Content is accurate, covers two important contribution.	Content is accurate, covers one important contribution.	Content is accurate but covers no important contributions.	Content not accurate and has no contributions.
Personal Connection	Descriptive and clear personal connection made to the content.	Personal connection made to the content.	Generic connection made to the content.	Vague personal connection made to the content.	No personal connection made to the content.
Authoritative	The website is authored by an authority in that area.	The website is a collection of other websites that are authoritative.	The website seems to have good content, but I can't tell who created the site.	The website was not created by authorities.	Hoax (or made up) website.

Student Name: _____

Discovery: _____

Day 1: Background Research

	4	3	2	1	0
Bookmarked Websites	5 or more bookmarks in Diigo created.	4 bookmarks in Diigo created.	3 bookmarks in Diigo created.	2 bookmarks in Diigo created.	1 or no bookmarks in Diigo created.
Diigo Notes	Content is accurate, covers four important facts.	Content is accurate, covers three important facts.	Content is accurate, covers two important facts.	Content is accurate, covers one important fact.	Content not accurate or has no facts.
Classroom Discussion	Student shares 2 important facts and listens to the ideas of others.	Student shares 2 important facts but doesn't always listen to the ideas of others.	Student shares 1 important fact and listens to the ideas of others.	Student shares 1 important fact but doesn't always listen to the ideas of others.	Student did not share or participate.

Day 2: Author Information

	4	3	2	1	0
Bookmarked Websites	5 or more bookmarks in Diigo created.	4 bookmarks in Diigo created.	3 bookmarks in Diigo created.	2 bookmarks in Diigo created.	1 or no bookmarks in Diigo created.
Diigo Notes	Content is accurate, covers four important facts.	Content is accurate, covers three important facts.	Content is accurate, covers two important facts.	Content is accurate, covers one important fact.	Content not accurate or has no facts.
Classroom Discussion	Student shares 2 important facts and listens to the ideas of others.	Student shares 2 important facts but doesn't always listen to the ideas of others.	Student shares 1 important fact and listens to the ideas of others.	Student shares 1 important fact but doesn't always listen to the ideas of others.	Student did not share or participate.

Appendix

Creating Videos with Jing

Download Jing

Go to the Jing website (/www.techsmith.com/Jing/) and download Jing. Jing is compatible with both Macs and PCs. You can download Jing unto any computer you want and use the same account for all computers. Jing is required to create videos and take screenshots but it is not required to watch the finished videos.

Manage Settings

Once you've set up your Jing account, you will see the Jing icon.

By default, Jing starts automatically every time you start your computer. Click on the **more** icon to change this setting.

Under **startup options,** you can unclick **launch at startup** or check if you want to hide the Jing sun. Here, you can also set up hot keys or manage your account. When finished, click the checkmark.

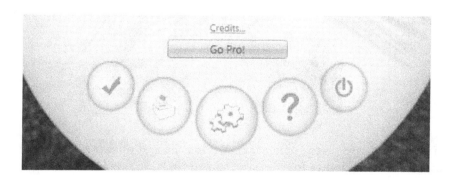

If the sun's location bothers you, simply click hold and drag it to a different part of the computer. Mine defaulted too far to the right and kept getting in the way of closing programs, so I moved it over to the left.

Things to Consider

Jing is a powerful creation tool for tutorials and step-by-step directions. Jing will capture your keystrokes and allow narration as you walk through step-by-step directions for completing tasks. Before you make a long video, check that the program is picking up your microphone and that you don't have a lot of background noise. I can't create Jing videos at my library because of the echo and students in the background. When watching your video, check to make sure that nothing is in the video that you don't want viewed by others. This includes any items that might be located on your computer such as bookmarks, files on your desktop, desktop images, and so on.

Finally, the videos that you create are on the Internet but they aren't indexed. That means that, in theory, you have to give the URL to someone for them to be able to view the website. Keep in mind, though, that if it's on the Internet, it could be viewed, so when a doing tutorial, use fake patron IDs instead of real patron IDs. But you could add these help videos to your jog, your LiveBinder, whatever!

History

The middle Jing sunray takes you to **History**, where you can see all videos and screenshots that you've updated. Click on the item you want to look at; you have three options. First, click the eye if you want to watch a video or look at a screenshot. Click the **Share** button to get the link.

It will actually take you to the website, just copy and paste the code in the address bar. The third option is deleting, if you no longer want that item. Once you delete it, you cannot get it back, so make sure you are deleting the correct one.

Capture Photos and Video

When you choose **capture**, you will see a set of crossbars that you can move in any direction. This sets the portion of your screen you will take a picture of or use for recording purposes. If it is grayed out, it will not show. Keep this in mind if you're doing an Internet tutorial, because your bookmark toolbar will be visible to everyone. You can always hide this toolbar before you start the project, as mentioned in the first chapter under "Bookmark Toolbar."

Photo Capture

In capture mode, you have several options. First, select the area of your screen for photo capture and then choose the option **Capture Image**. Next, add arrows, text, frames, or highlights as desired. Jing assigns a random file name to each capture. Change this to something that will make sense to you later. Other options for sharing the edited capture include:

- **Share via Screencast**—takes a picture that uploads and is viewable in your history. You will get a direct link to this image so you can make a QR code or link in a social bookmarking site.

- **Save**—to save locally on your computer.

- **Copy**—to make a copy so that you can paste into another document.

- **Edit in Snagit**—a link to a paid program that allows more editing features.

- **Cancel**—use this if you didn't get a good capture of the screen or do not want to save or share the image.

- On the left, you have options to add arrows, text, boxes, and highlights.

Video Capture

The second option in capture is for video capture. Select the area of your screen for video capture and then the menu options for video will appear. These options are very simple, but there is no editing feature in the free version, so set aside time to make a few mistakes. If you want to add voice, you will need a microphone of some kind.

Make sure when you are finished that you hit **stop** not **cancel** or you will lose your work. Once you hit **stop,** you can view the video and make a redo if needed. Jing assigns a random name. Change this to something that will make sense to you later. Video options include:

- **Share via Screencast**—uploads your video and is viewable in your history. You will get a direct link to this video, so you can make a QR code or link in a social bookmarking site. These display very nicely in LiveBinders but use as a link not as media.

- **Save**—to save locally on your computer.

- **Edit in Camtasia Studio**—a link to a paid program that allows more video editing features.

- **Cancel**—remember to only use **cancel** if you want to stop recording and start over entirely. Use **stop** if you are finished with the video and ready to save.

Resource List

Web 2.0 Websites for Social Bookmarking

Avos: www.avos.com

Delicious: www.delicious.com

Diigo: www.diigo.com

Jog the Web: www.jogtheweb.com

Kaywa QR Creator: http://qrcode.kaywa.com

Kayawa QR Code Reader: http://reader.kaywa.com

LaterThis: http://laterthis.com

Live Binders: www.livebinders.com

Sqworl: http://sqworl.com or mobile app http://sqworl.com/m

Tutorial Sites or Wikis

Delicious: http://blog.delicious.com/ and http://support.delicious.com/forum/categories.php

Diigo: http://help.diigo.com

Jog the Web: http://blog.jogtheweb.com

Kaywa QR Creator: http://support.kaywa.com/

Kaywa QR Reader: http://reader.kaywa.com/faq

LaterThis: http://laterthis.com/help or http://laterthis.uservoice.com/forums/3428-general

LiveBinders: www.livebinders.com/welcome/podcast or www.livebinders.wordpress.com/

Sqworl: http://sqworl.com/blog/

Supplemental Web 2.0 Websites

Animoto: http://animoto.com

Book Seer: http://bookseer.com

Book Trailers for All: http://booktrailersforall.com/

Booktrailers Movies for Literacy: www.homepages.dsu.edu/mgeary/booktrailers/

Bubble.us: www.bubbl.us.com

Digitalbooktalk: http://digitalbooktalk.com/

EasyBib: www.easybib.com

Edu.glogster: http://edu.glogster.com

Flickr Creative Commons: http://flickr.com/creativecommons

Glogster: www.glogster.com

Jing: www.techsmith.com/Jing/

Linoit: http://en.linoit.com/

MindMeister: www.mindmeister.com/

Morguefile: http://morguefile.com

Online Stopwatch: www.online-stopwatch.com/

PhotoPeach: http://photopeach.com

Pics4Learning: http://pics4learning.com

Pixenate: http://pixenate.com/SAILOn: www.pasadenaisd.org/sailon/

Survey Monkey: http://surveymonkey.com

Survey Tool: http://surveytool.com

Sweet Search: www.sweetsearch.com/

Tagxedo: www.tagxedo.com

Tiny URL: http://tinyurl.com

Wordle: www.wordle.net

Websites and Wikis with Ideas for Implementing Web 2.0 Strategies

Digital Goonies: http://digitalgoonies.com/

Ed.Tech: http://edte.ch/blog/?page_id=424

Edudemic: http://edudemic.com/

Library Campground: http://librarycampground.wikispaces.com/

Power Librarian: http://powerlibrarian.blogspot.com

Articles

Holland, Jim. "Issues with Web 2.0 Revised." *Web Application*. Available at: http://webapplications. wikispaces.com/. Accessed November 1, 2011.

Watters, Audrey. "Delicious has New Owners: YouTube Founders Chad Hurley and Steve Chen." *Read Write Web.com*. Available at: www.readwriteweb.com/archives/delicious_has_new_owners_ youtube_founders_chad_hur.php. Accessed July 6, 2011.

Glossary

Annotation—A comment or note on a page about the contained content.

App compatible—Social bookmarking site works on the computer or on a downloadable app.

Binder—Think file cabinet drawer. A collection of helpful links, documents, or text that relate to one topic.

Bookmark—A quick way to record websites you frequently use so you can access them easily and sort them logically.

Bookmarklet—A shortcut that you can add to your browser to make bookmarking easier.

Bookmark properties—Once you have bookmarked a website, if you right-click on the link, you will see a **properties** option. This will allow you to rename the shortcut, if you desire. Be sure to only change the name, not the location, or the shortcut won't work.

Bookmark toolbar—A bar on most browsers that allows you to drag and drop the websites you use most frequently, for easy reference.

Browser—The tool you use to locate and retrieve information on the Internet.

Browser-based app—This is not a downloadable app, but rather a browser that makes using a smart device easy, without excessive scrolling.

Cache—Stores your recently access data for quick retrieval at a later date.

Cloud—The ability to access your files no matter where you are, because you are storing them on a server that isn't connected to your computer (so it doesn't take any of your computer's storage space).

Common Core Standards—Standards for what students are expected to learn, to prepare them for college and careers.

Concept map—A visual way to organize bookmarks or content.

E-mail verification—Requires that the person creating an account log into their e-mail and click a secure link before accessing an account.

Embed—Allows you to add code that links your page to information stored on another website.

Export—Taking information from one area and saving it for later use. In this case, saving bookmarks onto a desktop.

Flash—A program that adds movement and animation to still images.

Frames—Reduce the size of the website so that the entire website is contained within the structure of another website.

Homepage—A page you create that contains the items you use most frequently.

Import—Taking information from one area and adding it into another.

Personal Learning Network—A group of individuals that you follow to learn more about an area of interest or stay current in your profession.

Properties—Basic settings you can control in social bookmarking sites, such as name, description, etc.

QR code—A 2D barcode that contains basic information, such as a link to a website, contact information, or a phone number.

QR code reader—An app that you use to read a QR code (requires a smart device or computer and must have a camera).

Social bookmarking—Bookmarking websites on the Internet and collaborating and sharing ideas.

Social networking—Connecting with individuals electronically for personal or professional correspondence.

Sorting hierarchy—The ability to sort the links and user-created material into the order that will work best for the needs of your project by using the up and down arrows.

Static—Does not change. For example, I can create a QR code to link patrons to a website. Because the link is static and only the content changes, I do not need to update the QR code.

Subtab—Two or more websites within a tab that are on a related topic.

Tab—Think file folder. It is a page that holds a direct link to a website or introductory information with subtabs.

Tag—A one- or two-word category that describes a website. Each website may reflect multiple tags.

URL—The specific address of a website.

Web Content—This is content that you get directly from the Internet. These are the websites you are going to bookmark.

Web 2.0—A more interactive form of the Internet that involves collaboration rather than just statically providing information.

Widget—Code you get when you create content on one website but want to embed or place that content directly onto your website without taking up space on your server.

Index

About the Author

ALICIA VANDENBROEK is a librarian at Shackelford Junior High, where she was previously awarded Teacher of the Year by her peers. Before graduating with her MLS from the University of North Texas, Alicia was an elementary school teacher. She has had three articles published in *Library Media Connection*, but this is her first book.

www.ingramcontent.com/pod-product-compliance
Lightning Source LLC
Chambersburg PA
CBHW060136060326
40690CB00018B/3900